Oliver Optic, Shepard Lee and

Now or Never

The Adventures of Bobby Bright - A Story for Young Folks

Oliver Optic, Shepard Lee and

Now or Never
The Adventures of Bobby Bright - A Story for Young Folks

ISBN/EAN: 9783337155896

Printed in Europe, USA, Canada, Australia, Japan

Cover: Foto ©Thomas Meinert / pixelio.de

More available books at **www.hansebooks.com**

NOW OR NEVER

OF

THE ADVENTURES

OF

BOBBY BRIGHT

A STORY FOR YOUNG FOLKS.

BY

OLIVER OPTIC

AUTHOR OF "THE BOAT CLUB," "ALL ABOARD"
"IN DOORS AND OUT," ETC.

BOSTON
LEE AND SHEPARD PUBLISHERS
CHARLES T. DILLINGHAM NEW YORK

Entered, according to Act of Congress, in the year 1855, by
WILLIAM T. ADAMS,
In the Clerk's Office of the District Court of the District of Massachusetts.

Copyright, 1884,
By WILLIAM T. ADAMS.

TO MY NEPHEW

CHARLES HENRY POPE,

This Book

IS AFFECTIONATELY DEDICATED.

PREFACE.

THE story contained in this volume is a record of youthful struggles, not only in the world without, but in the world within; and the success of the little hero is not merely a gathering up of wealth and honors, but a triumph over the temptations that beset the pilgrim on the plain of life. The attainment of worldly prosperity is not the truest victory; and the author has endeavored to make the interest of his story depend more on the hero's devotion to principles than on his success in business.

Bobby Bright is a smart boy; perhaps the reader will think he is altogether too smart for one of his years. This is a progressive age, and any thing which Young America may do need not surprise any person. That little gentleman is older than his father, knows more than his mother, can talk politics, smoke cigars, and drive a 2 : 40 horse. He orders "one stew" with as much ease as a man of forty, and can even pronounce correctly the villanous names of sundry French and German wines and liqueurs. One would suppose, to hear him talk, that he had been intimate with Socrates and Solon, with Napoleon and Noah Webster; in short, that whatever he did not know was not worth knowing.

In the face of these manifestations of exuberant genius, it would be absurd to accuse the author of making his hero do too much. All he has done is to give this genius a right direction; and for politics, cigars, 2:40 horses, and "one stew," he has substituted the duties of a rational and accountable being, regarding them as better fitted to develop the young gentleman's mind, heart, and soul.

Bobby Bright is something more than a smart boy. He is a good boy, and makes a true man. His daily life is the moral of the story, and the author hopes that his devotion to principle will make a stronger impression upon the mind of the young reader, than even the most exciting incidents of his eventful career.

WILLIAM T. ADAMS.

DORCHESTER, Nov. 15, 1856.

CONTENTS.

                                                                         PAGE

CHAP. I. — In which Bobby goes a fishing, and catches a Horse. 11

CHAP. II. — In which Bobby blushes several Times, and does a Sum in Arithmetic. 22

CHAP. III. — In which the Little Black House is bought, but not paid for. 33

CHAP. IV. — In which Bobby gets out of one Scrape, and into another. 43

CHAP. V. — In which Bobby gives his Note for Sixty Dollars. 55

CHAP. VI. — In which Bobby sets out on his Travels. . . 67

CHAP. VII. — In which Bobby stands up for certain "Inalienable Rights." 77

CHAP. VIII. — In which Mr. Timmins is astonished, and Bobby dines in Chestnut Street. 88

CHAP. IX. — In which Bobby opens various Accounts, and wins his first Victory. 98

CHAP. X. — In which Bobby is a little too smart. . . . 111

CONTENTS.

CHAP. XI. — In which Bobby strikes a Balance, and returns to Riverdale. 123

CHAP. XII. — In which Bobby astonishes sundry Persons, and pays Part of his Note. 134

CHAP. XIII. — In which Bobby declines a Copartnership, and visits B—— again. 148

CHAP. XIV. — In which Bobby's Air Castle is upset, and Tom Spicer takes to the Woods. 163

CHAP. XV — In which Bobby gets into a Scrape, and Tom Spicer turns up again. 175

CHAP. XVI. — In which Bobby finds "it is an ill wind that blows no one any good." 187

CHAP. XVII. — In which Tom has a good Time, and Bobby meets with a terrible Misfortune. 193

CHAP. XVIII. — In which Bobby takes French Leave, and camps in the Woods. 213

CHAP. XIX. — In which Bobby has a narrow Escape, and goes to Sea with Sam Ray. 225

CHAP. XX. — In which the Clouds blow over, and Bobby is himself again. 239

CHAP. XXI. — In which Bobby steps off the Stage, and the Author must finish "Now or Never." 254

NOW OR NEVER.

NOW OR NEVER;

OR,

THE ADVENTURES OF BOBBY BRIGHT.

CHAPTER I.

IN WHICH BOBBY GOES A FISHING, AND CATCHES A HORSE.

"By jolly! I've got a bite!" exclaimed Tom Spicer, a rough, hard-looking boy, who sat on a rock by the river's side, anxiously watching the cork float on his line.

"Catch him, then," quietly responded Bobby Bright, who occupied another rock near the first speaker, as he pulled up a large pout, and, without any appearance of exultation, proceeded to unhook and place him in his basket.

"You are a lucky dog, Bob," added Tom, as he glanced into the basket of his companion, which now contained six good-sized fishes. "I haven't caught one yet."

"You don't fish deep enough."

"I fish on the bottom."

"That is too deep."

"It don't make any difference how I fish; it is all luck."

"Not all luck, Tom; there is something in doing it right."

"I shall not catch a fish," continued Tom, in despair.

"You'll catch something else, though, when you go home."

"Will I?"

"I'm afraid you will."

"Who says I will?"

"Didn't you tell me you were 'hooking jack'?"

"Who is going to know any thing about it?"

"The master will know you are absent."

"I shall tell him my mother sent me over to the village on an errand."

"I never knew a fellow to 'hook jack,' yet, without getting found out."

"I shall not get found out unless you blow on me; and you wouldn't be mean enough to do that;" and Tom glanced uneasily at his companion.

"Suppose your mother should ask me if I had seen you."

"You would tell her you have not, of course."

"Of course?"

"Why, wouldn't you? Wouldn't you do as much as that for a fellow?"

"It would be a lie."

"A lie! Humph!"

"I wouldn't lie for any fellow," replied Bobby stoutly, as he pulled in his seventh fish, and placed him in the basket.

"Wouldn't you?"

"No, I wouldn't."

"Then let me tell you this; if you peach on me I'll smash your head."

Tom Spicer removed one hand from the fish pole and, doubling his fist, shook it with energy at hi companion.

"Smash away," replied Bobby, coolly. "I shall not go out of my way to tell tales; but if your mother or the master asks me the question, I shall not lie."

"Won't you?"

"No, I won't."

"I'll bet you will;" and Tom dropped his fish pole, and was on the point of jumping over to the rock occupied by Bobby, when the float of the former disappeared beneath the surface of the water.

"You have got a bite," coolly interposed Bobby, pointing to the line.

Tom snatched the pole, and with a violent twitch, pulled up a big pout; but his violence jerked the hook out of the fish's mouth, and he disappeared beneath the surface of the river.

"Just my luck!" muttered Tom.

"Keep cool, then."

"I will fix you yet."

"All right; but you had better not let go your pole again, or you will lose another fish."

"I'm bound to smash your head, though."

"No, you won't."

"Won't I?'"

"Two can play at that game."

"Do you stump me?"

"No; I don't want to fight; I won't fight if I can help it."

"I'll bet you won't!" sneered Tom.

"But I will defend myself."

"Humph!"

"I am not a liar, and the fear of a flogging shall not make me tell a lie."

"Go to Sunday school — don't you?"

"I do; and besides that, my mother always taugh me never to tell a lie."

"Come! you needn't preach to me. By and by, you will call me a liar."

"No, I won't; but just now you told me you meant to lie to your mother, and to the master."

"What if I did? That is none of your business."

"It *is* my business when you want me to lie for you, though; and I shall not do it."

"Blow on me, and see what you will get."

"I don't mean to blow on you."

"Yes you do."

"I will not lie about it; that's all."

"By jolly! see that horse!" exclaimed Tom, suddenly, as he pointed to the road leading to Riverdale centre.

"By gracious!" added Bobby, dropping his fish pole, as he saw the horse running at a furious rate up the road from the village.

The mad animal was attached to a chaise, in which was seated a lady, whose frantic shrieks pierced the soul of our youthful hero.

The course of the road was by the river's side for nearly half a mile, and crossed the stream at a wooden bridge but a few rods from the place where the boys were fishing.

Bobby Bright's impulses were noble and generous; and without stopping to consider the peril to which the attempt would expose him, he boldly resolved to stop that horse, or let the animal dash him to pieces on the bridge.

"Now or never!" shouted he, as he leaped from the rock, and ran with all his might to the bridge.

The shrieks of the lady rang in his ears, and seemed to command him, with an authority which he could not resist, to stop the horse. There was no time for deliberation; and, indeed, Bobby did not want any deliberation. The lady was in danger; if the horse's flight was not checked, she would be dashed in pieces; and what then could excuse him for neglecting his duty? Not the fear of broken limbs, of mangled flesh, or even of a sudden and violent death.

It is true Bobby did not think of any of these things; though, if he had, it would have made no difference with him. He was a boy who would not fight except in self defence, but he had the courage to do a deed which might have made the stoutest heart tremble with terror.

Grasping a broken rail as he leaped over the fence, he planted himself in the middle of the bridge, which was not more than half as wide as the road at each end of it, to await the coming of the furious animal. On he came, and the piercing shrieks of the affrighted lady nerved him to the performance of his perilous duty.

The horse approached him at a mad run, and his feet struck the loose planks of the bridge. The brave boy then raised his big club, and brandished it with all his might in the air. Probably the horse did not mean any thing very bad; was only frightened, and had no wicked intentions towards the lady; so that when a new danger menaced him in front, he stopped suddenly, and with so much violence as to throw the lady forward from her seat upon the dasher of the chaise. He gave a long snort, which was his way of expressing his fear. He was evidently astonished at the sudden barrier to his further progress, and commenced running back.

"Save me!" screamed the lady.

"I will, ma'am; don't be scared!" replied Bobby, confidently, as he dropped his club, and grasped the bridle of the horse, just as he was on the point of whirling round to escape by the way he had come.

"Stop him! Do stop him!" cried the lady.

"Whoa!" said Bobby, in gentle tones, as he patted the trembling horse on his neck. "Whoa, good horse! Be quiet! Whoa!"

The animal, in his terror kept running backward and forward; but Bobby persevered in his gentle treatment, and finally soothed him, so that he stood quiet enough for the lady to get out of the chaise

"What a miracle that I am alive!" exclaimed she when she realized that she stood once more upon the firm earth.

"Yes, ma'am, it is lucky he didn't break the chaise Whoa! Good horse! Stand quiet!"

"What a brave little fellow you are!" said the lady, as soon as she could recover her breath so as to express her admiration of Bobby's bold act.

"O, I don't mind it," replied he, blushing like a rose in June. "Did he run away with you?"

"No; my father left me in the chaise for a moment while he went into a store in the village, and a teamster who was passing by snapped his whip, which frightened Kate so that she started off at the top of her speed. I was so terrified, that I screamed with all my might, which frightened her the more. The more I screamed, the faster she ran."

"I dare say. Good horse! Whoa, Kate!"

"She is a splendid creature; she never did such a thing before. My father will think I am killed."

By this time, Kate had become quite reasonable, and seemed very much obliged to Bobby for preventing her from doing mischief to her mistress; for she looked at the lady with a glance of satisfaction, which her deliverer interpreted as a promise to behave better in future. He relaxed his grasp upon the bridle, patted her upon the neck, and said sundry pleasant things to encourage her in her assumed purpose of doing better. Kate appeared to understand Bobby's kind words, and declared as plainly as a horse could declare that she would be sober and tractable.

"Now, ma'am, if you will get into the chaise again, I think Kate will let me drive her down to the village."

"O, dear! I should not dare to do so."

"Then, if you please, I will drive down alone, so as to let your father know that you are safe."

"Do."

"I am sure he must feel very bad, and I may save him a great deal of pain, for a man can suffer a great deal in a very short time."

"You are a little philosopher, as well as a hero, and if you are not afraid of Kate, you may do as you wish."

"She seems very gentle now;" and Bobby turned her round, and got into the chaise.

" Be very careful," said the lady.

" I will."

Bobby took the reins, and Kate, true to the promise she had virtually made, started off at a round pace towards the village.

He had not gone more than a quarter of a mile of the distance when he met a wagon containing three men, one of whom was the lady's father. The gestures which he made assured Bobby he had found the person whom he sought, and he stopped.

" My daughter! Where is she?" gasped the gentleman, as he leaped from the wagon.

" She is safe, sir," replied Bobby, with all the enthusiasm of his warm nature.

" Thank God!" added the gentleman, devoutly as he placed himself in the chaise by the side of Bobby.

CHAPTER II.

IN WHICH BOBBY BLUSHES SEVERAL TIMES, AND DOES A SUM IN ARITHMETIC.

Mr. Bayard, the owner of the horse, and the father of the lady whom Bobby had saved from impending death, was too much agitated to say much, even to the bold youth who had rendered him such a signal service. He could scarcely believe the intelligence which the boy brought him; it seemed too good to be true. He had assured himself that Ellen — for that was the young lady's name — was killed, or dreadfully injured.

Kate was driven at the top of her speed, and in a few moments reached the bridge, where Ellen was awaiting his arrival.

"Here I am, father, alive and unhurt!" cried Ellen, as Mr. Bayard stopped the horse.

"Thank Heaven my child!" replied the glad

father, embracing his daughter. "I was sure you were killed."

"No, father; thanks to this bold youth, I an. uninjured."

"I am under very great obligations to you, young man," continued Mr. Bayard, grasping Bobby's hand.

"O, never mind, sir;" and Bobby blushed just as he had blushed when the young lady spoke to him.

"We shall never forget you — shall we, father?" added Ellen.

"No, my child; and I shall endeavor to repay, to some slight extent, our indebtedness to him. But you have not yet told me how you were saved."

"O, I merely stopped the horse; that's all," answered Bobby, modestly.

"Yes, father, but he placed himself right before Kate when she was almost flying over the ground. When I saw him, I was certain that he would lose his life, or be horribly mangled for his boldness," interposed Ellen.

"It was a daring deed, young man, to place yourself before an affrighted horse in that manner," said Mr. Bayard.

"I didn't mind it. sir."

"And then he flourished a big club, almost as big as he is himself, in the air, which made Kate pause in her mad career, when my deliverer here grasped her by the bit and held her."

"It was well and bravely done."

"That it was, father; not many men would have been bold enough to do what he did," added Ellen, with enthusiasm.

"Very true; and I feel that I am indebted to him for your safety. What is your name, young man?"

"Robert Bright, sir."

Mr. Bayard took from his pocket several pieces of gold, which he offered to Bobby.

"No, I thank you, sir," replied Bobby, blushing.

"What! as proud as you are bold?"

"I don't like to be paid for doing my duty."

"Bravo! You are a noble little fellow! But you must take this money, not as a reward for what you have done, but as a testimonial of my gratitude."

"I would rather not, sir."

"Do take it, Robert," added Ellen.

"I don't like to take it. It looks mean to take money for doing one's duty."

"Take it, Robert, to please me;" and the young lady smiled so sweetly that Bobby's resolution began to give way. "Only to please me, Robert."

"I will, to please you; but I don't feel right about it."

"You must not be too proud, Robert," said Mr. Bayard, as he put the gold pieces into his hand.

"I am not proud, sir; only I don't like to be paid for doing my duty."

"Not paid, my young friend. Consider that you have placed me under an obligation to you for life. This money is only an expression of my own and my daughter's feelings. It is but a small sum, but I hope you will permit me to do something more for you, when you need it. You will regard me as your friend as long as you live."

"Thank you, sir."

"When you want any assistance of any kind, come to me. I live in Boston; here is my business card."

Mr. Bayard handed him a card, on which Bobby read, " F. Bayard & Co., Booksellers and Publishers, No. — Washington Street, Boston."

"You are very kind, sir."

"I want you should come to Boston and see us too," interposed Ellen. "I should be delighted to show you the city, to take you to the Athenæum and the Museum."

"Thank you."

Mr. Bayard inquired of Bobby about his parents, where he lived, and about the circumstances of his family. He then took out his memorandum book, in which he wrote the boy's name and residence.

"I am sorry to leave you now, Robert, but I have over twenty miles to ride to-day. I should be glad to visit your mother, and next time I come to Riverdale, I shall certainly do so."

"Thank you, sir; my mother is a very poor woman, but she will be glad to see you."

"Now, good by, Robert."

"Good by," repeated Ellen.

"Good by."

Mr. Bayard drove off, leaving Bobby standing on the bridge with the gold pieces in his hand.

"Here's luck!" said Bobby, shaking the coin. "Won't mother's eyes stick out when she sees these shiners? There are no such shiners in the river as these.

Bobby was astonished, and the more he gazed a he gold pieces, the more bewildered he became. He had never held so much money in his hand before. There were three large coins and one smaller one. He turned them over and over, and finally ascertained that the large coins were ten dollar pieces, and the smaller one a five dollar piece. Bobby was not a great scholar, but he knew enough of arithmetic to calculate the value of his treasure. He was so excited, however, that he did not arrive at the conclusion half so quick as most of my young readers would have done.

"Thirty-five dollars!" exclaimed Bobby, when the problem was solved. "Gracious!"

"Hallo, Bob!" shouted Tom Spicer, who had got tired of fishing; besides, the village clock was just striking twelve, and it was time for him to go home.

Bobby made no answer, but hastily tying the gold pieces up in the corner of his handkerchief, he threw the broken rail he had used in stopping the horse where it belonged, and started for the place where he had left his fishing apparatus.

"Hallo, Bob!"

"Well, Tom?"

"Stopped him — didn't you?"

"I did."

"You were a fool; he might have killed you."

"So he might; but I didn't stop to think of that. The lady's life was in danger."

"What of that?"

"Every thing, I should say."

"Did he give you any thing?"

"Yes;" and Bobby continued his walk down to the river's side.

"I say, what did he give you, Bobby?" persisted Tom, following him.

"O, he gave me a good deal of money."

"How much?"

"I want to get my fish line now; I will tell you all about it some other time," replied Bobby, who rather suspected the intentions of his companion.

"Tell me now; how much was it?"

"Never mind it now."

"Humph! Do you think I mean to rob you?"

"No."

"Ain't you going halveses?"

"Why should I?"

"Wasn't I with you?"

"Were you?"

"Wasn't I fishing with you?"

"You did not do any thing about stopping the noise."

"I would, if I hadn't been afraid to go up to the road."

"Afraid?"

"Somebody might have seen me, and they would have known that I was hooking jack."

"Then you ought not to share the money."

"Yes, I had. When a fellow is with you, he ought to have half. It is mean not to give him half."

"If you had done any thing to help stop the horse, I would have shared with you. But you didn't."

"What of that?"

Bobby was particularly sensitive in regard to the charge of meanness. His soul was a great deal bigger than his body, and he was always generous, even to his own injury, among his companions. It was evident to him that Tom had no claim to any part of the reward; but he could not endure the thought even of being accused of meanness.

"I'll tell you what I will do, if you think I ought to share with you. I will leave it out to Squire Lee; and if he thinks you ought to have half, or any part of the money, I will give it to you."

"No, you don't; you want to get me into a scrape for hooking jack. I see what you are up to."

"I will state the case to him without telling him who the boys are."

"No, you don't! You want to be mean about it. Come, hand over half the money."

"I will not," replied Bobby, who, when it became a matter of compulsion, could stand his ground at any peril.

"How much have you got?"

"Thirty-five dollars."

"By jolly! And you mean to keep it all yourself?"

"I mean to give it to my mother."

"No, you won't! If you are going to be mean about it, I'll smash your head!"

This was a favorite expression with Tom Spicer,

who was a noted bully among the boys of Riverdale.
The young ruffian now placed himself in front of
Bobby, and shook his clinched fist in his face.

"Hand over."

"No, I won't. You have no claim to any part of
the money; at least, I think you have not. If you
have a mind to leave it out to Squire Lee, I will do
what is right about it."

"Not I; hand over, or I'll smash your head!"

"Smash away," replied Bobby, placing himself on
the defensive.

"Do you think you can lick me?" asked Tom not
a little embarrassed by this exhibition of resolution
on the part of his companion.

"I don't think any thing about it; but you don't
bully me in that kind of style."

"Won't I?"

"No."

But Tom did not immediately put his threat in
execution, and Bobby would not be the aggressor; so
he stepped one side to pass his assailant. Tom took
this as an evidence of the other's desire to escape, and
struck him a heavy blow on the side of the head.

The next instant the bully was floundering in the soft mud of a ditch; Bobby's reply was more than Tom had bargained for, and while he was dragging himself out of the ditch, our hero ran down to the river, and got his fish pole and basket.

"You'll catch it for that!" growled Tom.

"I'm all ready, whenever it suits your convenience," replied Bobby.

"Just come out here and take it in fair fight," continued Tom, who could not help bullying, even in the midst of his misfortune.

"No, I thank you; I don't want to fight with any fellow. I will not fight if I can help it."

"What did you hit me for, then?"

"In self-defence."

"Just come out here, and try it fair?"

"No;" and Bobby hurried home, leaving the bully astonished and discomfited by the winding up of the morning's sport.

CHAPTER III.

IN WHICH THE LITTLE BLACK HOUSE IS BOUGHT BUT NOT PAID FOR.

PROBABLY my young readers have by this time come to the conclusion that Bobby Bright was a very clever fellow — one whose acquaintance they would be happy to cultivate. Perhaps by this time they have become so far interested in him as to desire to know who his parents were, what they did, and in what kind of a house he lived.

I hope none of my young friends will think any less of him when I inform them that Bobby lived in an old black house which had never been painted, which had no flower garden in front of it, and which, in a word, was quite far from being a palace. A great many very nice city folks would not have considered it fit to live in, would have turned up their noses at it, and wondered that any human beings could be so degraded as to live in such a miserable house. But the widow Bright, Bobby's mother, thought it was a very comfortable house, and considered herself very fortunate in being able to get so good a dwelling. She had never lived in a fine house, knew nothing about velvet carpets, mirrors seven feet high, damask chairs and lounges, or any of the smart things which very rich and very proud city people consider absolutely necessary for their comfort. Her father had been a poor man, her husband had died a poor man, and her own life had been a struggle to keep the demons of poverty and want from invading her humble abode.

Mr. Bright, her deceased husband, had been a day laborer in Riverdale. He never got more than a dollar a day, which was then considered very good wages in the country. He was a very honest, industrious man, and while he lived, his family did very well. Mrs. Bright was a careful, prudent woman, and helped him support the family. They never knew what it was to want for any thing.

Poor people, as well as rich, have an ambition to be something which they are not, or to have something which they have not. Every person, who has any energy of character, desires to get ahead in the world. Some merchants, who own big ships and big warehouses by the dozen, desire to be what they consider rich. But their idea of wealth is very grand. They wish to count it in millions of dollars, in whole blocks of warehouses; and they are even more discontented than the day laborer who has to earn his dinner before he can eat it.

Bobby's father and mother had just such an ambition, only it was so modest that the merchant would have laughed at it. They wanted to own the little black house in which they resided, so that they could not only be sure of a home while they lived, but have the satisfaction of living in their own house. This was a very reasonable ideal, compared with that of the rich merchants I have mentioned; but it was even more difficult for them to reach it, for the wages were small, and they had many mouths to feed.

Mr. Bright had saved up fifty dollars; and he thought a great deal more of this sum than many people do of a thousand dollars. He had had to work very hard and be very prudent in order to accumulate this sum, which made him value it all the more highly.

With this sum of fifty dollars at his command, John Bright felt rich; and then, more than ever before, he wanted to own the little black house. He felt as grand as a lord; and as soon as the forty-nine dollars had become fifty, he waited upon Mr. Hardhand, a little crusty old man, who owned the little black house, and proposed to purchase it.

The landlord was a hard man. Every body in Riverdale said he was mean and stingy. Any generous-hearted man would have been willing to make an easy bargain with an honest, industrious, poor man, like John Bright, who wished to own the house in which he lived; but Mr. Hardhand, although he was rich, only thought how he could make more money. He asked the poor man four hundred dollars for the old house and the little lot of land on which it stood.

It was a matter of great concern to John Bright. Four hundred dollars was a " mint of money," and he could not see how he should ever be able to save so much from his daily earnings. So he talked with Squire Lee about it, who told him that three hundred was all it was worth. John offered this for it, and after a month's hesitation, Mr Hardhand accepted th offer, agreeing to take fifty dollars down, and the rest in semi-annual payments of twenty-five dollars each, until the whole was paid.

I am thus particular in telling my readers about the bargain, because this debt which his father contracted was the means of making a man of Bobby, as will be seen in his subsequent history.

John Bright paid the first fifty dollars; but before the next instalment became due, the poor man was laid in his cold and silent grave. A malignant disease carried him off, and the hopes of the Bright family seemed to be blasted.

Four children were left to the widow. The youngest was only three years old, and Bobby, the oldest, was nine, when his father died. Squire Lee, who had always been a good friend of John Bright, told the widow that she had better go to the poorhouse, and not attempt to struggle along with such a fearful odds against her. But the widow nobly refused to become a pauper, and to make paupers of her children, whom she loved quite as much as though she and they had been born in a ducal palace. She told the squire that she had two hands, and as long as she had her health, the town need not trouble itself about her support.

Squire Lee was filled with surprise and admiration at the noble resolution of the poor woman; and when he returned to his house, he immediately sent her a cord of wood, ten bushels of potatoes, two bags of meal, and a firkin of salt pork.

The widow was very grateful for these articles, and no false pride prevented her from accepting the gift of her rich and kind-hearted neighbor.

Riverdale centre was largely engaged in the manufacturing of boots and shoes, and this business gave employment to a large number of men and women.

Mrs. Bright had for several years " closed " shoes — which, my readers who do not live in " shoe towns " may not know, means sewing or stitching them. To this business she applied herself with renewed energy. There was a large hotel in Riverdale centre, where several families from Boston spent the summer. By the aid of Squire Lee, she obtained the washing of these families, which was more profitable than closing shoes.

By these means she not only supported her family

very comfortably, but was able to save a little money towards paying for the house. Mr. Hardhand, by the persuasions of Squire Lee, had consented to let the widow keep the house, and pay for it as she could.

John Bright had been dead four years at the time we introduce Bobby to the reader. Mrs. Bright had paid another hundred dollars towards the house, with the interest; so there was now but one hundred due Bobby had learned to " close," and helped his mother a great deal; but the confinement and the stooping posture did not agree with his health, and his mother was obliged to dispense with his assistance. But the devoted little fellow found a great many ways of helping her. He was now thirteen, and was as handy about the house as a girl. When he was not better occupied, he would often go to the river and catch a mess of fish, which was so much clear gain.

The winter which had just passed had brought a great deal of sickness to the little black house. The children all had the measles, and two of them the scarlet fever, so that Mrs. Bright could not work much. Her affairs were not in a very prosperous condition when the spring opened; but the future was bright, and the widow, trusting in Providence, believed that all would end well.

One thing troubled her. She had not been able to save any thing for Mr. Hardhand. She could only pay her interest; but she hoped by the first of July to give him twenty-five dollars of the principal. But the first of July came, and she had only five dollars of the sum she had partly promised her creditor. She could not so easily recover from the disasters of the hard winter, and she had but just paid off the little debts she had contracted. She was nervous and uneasy as the day approached. Mr. Hardhand always abused her when she told him she could not pay him, and she dreaded his coming.

It was the first of July on which Bobby caught those pouts, caught the horse, and on which Tom Spicer had "caught a Tartar."

Bobby hastened home, as we said at the conclusion of the last chapter. He was as happy as a lord. He had fish enough in his basket for dinner, and for breakfast the next morning, and money enough in his pocket to make his mother as happy as a queen, if queens are always happy.

The widow Bright, though she had worried and fretted night and day about the money which was to be paid to Mr. Hardhand on the first of July, had not told her son any thing about it. It would only make him unhappy, she reasoned, and it was needless to make the dear boy miserable for nothing; so Bobby ran home all unconscious of the pleasure which was in store for him.

When he reached the front door, as he stopped to scrape his feet on the sharp stone there, as all considerate boys who love their mothers do, before they go into the house, he heard the angry tones of Mr. Hardhand. He was scolding and abusing his mother because she could not pay him the twenty-five dollars.

Bobby's blood boiled with indignation, and his first impulse was to serve him as he had served Tom Spicer, only a few moments before; but Bobby, as we have before intimated, was a peaceful boy, and not disposed to quarrel with any person; so he contented himself with muttering a few hard words.

"The wretch! What business has he to talk to my

mother in that style?" said he to himself. "I have a great mind to kick him out of the house."

But Bobby's better judgment came to his aid; and perhaps he realized that he and his mother would only get kicked out in return. He could battle with Mr. Hardhand, but not with the power which his wealth gave him; so, like a great many older persons in similar circumstances, he took counsel of prudence rather than impulse.

"Bear ye one another's burdens," saith the Scripture; but Bobby was not old enough or astute enough to realize that Mr. Hardhand's burden was his wealth, his love of money; that it made him little better than a Hottentot; and he could not feel as charitably towards him as a Christian should towards his erring, weak brother.

Setting his pole by the door, he entered the room where Hardhand was abusing his mother.

CHAPTER IV.

IN WHICH BOBBY GETS OUT OF ONE SCRAPE, AND INTO ANOTHER.

BOBBY was so indignant at the conduct of Mr Hardhand, that he entirely forgot the adventure of the morning; and he did not even think of the gold he had in his pocket. He loved his mother; he knew how hard she had worked for him and his brother and sisters; that she had burned the "midnight oil" at her clamps; and it made him feel very bad to near her abused as Mr. Hardhand was abusing her. It was not her fault that she had not the money to pay him. She had been obliged to spend a large portion of her time over the sick beds of her children, so that she could not earn so much money as usual; while the family expenses were necessarily much greater.

Bobby knew also that Mr. Hardhand was aware of

all the circumstances of his mother's position, and the more he considered the case the more brutal and inhuman was his course.

As our hero entered the family room with the basket of fish on his arm, the little crusty old man fixed the glance of his evil eye upon him.

"There is that boy, marm, idling away his time by the river, and eating you out of house and home," said the wretch. "Why don't you set him to work, and make him earn something?"

"Bobby is a very good boy," meekly responded the widow Bright.

"Humph! I should think he was. A great lazy lubber like him, living on his mother!" and Mr. Hardhand looked contemptuously at Bobby.

"I am not a lazy lubber," interposed the insulted boy with spirit.

"Yes, you are. Why don't you go to werk?"

"I do work."

"No, you don't; you waste your time paddling in the river."

"I don't."

"You had better teach this boy manners too, marm,'

said the creditor, who, like all men of small souls, was willing to take advantage of the power which the widow's indebtedness gave him. "He is saucy."

"I should like to know who taught *you* manners, Mr. Hardhand," replied Bobby, whose indignation was rapidly getting the better of his discretion.

"What!" growled Mr. Hardhand, aghast at this unwonted boldness.

"I heard what you said before I came in; and no decent man would go to the house of a poor woman to insult her."

"Humph! Mighty fine," snarled the little old man, his gray eyes twinkling with malice.

"Don't Bobby; don't be saucy to the gentleman," interposed his mother.

"Saucy, marm? You ought to horsewhip him for it. If you don't, I will."

"No, you won't!" replied Bobby, shaking his head significantly. "I can take care of myself."

"Did any one ever hear such impudence!" gasped Mr. Hardhand.

"Don't, Bobby, don't," pleaded the anxious mother.

"I should like to know what right you have to come here and abuse my mother," continued Bobby, who could not restrain his anger.

"Your mother owes me money, and she don't pay it, you young scoundrel!" answered Mr. Hardhand, foaming with rage.

"That is no reason why you should insult her. You can call *me* what you please, but you shall not insult my mother while I'm round."

"Your mother is a miserable woman, and ——"

"Say that again, and though you are an old man, I'll hit you for it. I'm big enough to protect my mother, and I'll do it."

Bobby doubled up his fists and edged up to Mr. Hardhand, fully determined to execute his threat if he repeated the offensive expression, or any other of a similar import. He was roused to the highest pitch of anger, and felt as though he had just as lief die as live in defence of his mother's good name.

I am not sure that I could excuse Bobby's violence under any other circumstances. He loved his mother — as the novelists would say, he idolized her; and Mr. Hardhand had certainly applied some very offensive epithets to her — epithets which no good son could calmly hear applied to a mother. Besides, Bobby, though his heart was a large one, and was in the right place, had never been educated into these nice distinctions of moral right and wrong which control the judgment of wise and learned men. He had an idea that violence, resistance with blows, was allowable in certain extreme cases; and he could conceive of no greater provocation than an insult to his mother.

"Be calm, Bobby; you are in a passion," said Mrs. Bright.

"I am surprised, marm," began Mr. Hardhand, who prudently refrained from repeating the offensive language — and I have no doubt he was surprised; for he looked both astonished and alarmed. "This boy has a most ungovernable temper."

"Don't you worry about my temper, Mr. Hardhand; I'll take care of myself. All I want of you is not to insult my mother. You may say what you like to me; but don't you call her hard names."

Mr. Hardhand, like all mean, little men, was a coward; and he was effectually intimidated by the bold and manly conduct of the boy. He changed his tone and manner at once.

"You have no money for me, marm?" said he, edging towards the door.

"No, sir; I am sorry to say that I have been able to save only five dollars since I paid you last; but I hope ——"

"Never mind, marm, never mind; I shall not trouble myself to come here again, where I am liable to be kicked by this ill-bred cub. No, marm, I shall not come again. Let the law take its course."

"O, mercy! See what you have brought upon us, Bobby," exclaimed Mrs. Bright, bursting into tears.

"Yes, marm, let the law take its course."

"O Bobby! Stop a moment, Mr. Hardhand; do stop a moment."

"Not a moment, marm. We'll see;" and Mr. Hardhand placed his hand upon the latch string.

Bobby felt very uneasy, and very unhappy at that moment. His passion had subsided, and he realized that he had done a great deal of mischief by his impetuous conduct.

Then the remembrance of his morning adventure

on the bridge came like a flash of sunshine to his
mind, and he eagerly drew from his pocket the handkerchief in which he had deposited the precious gold,
- doubly precious now, because it would enable him
to retrieve the error into which he had fallen, and do
something towards relieving his mother's embarrassment. With a trembling hand he untied the knot
which secured the money.

"Here, mother, here is thirty-five dollars;" and
he placed it in her hand.

"Why, Bobby!" exclaimed Mrs. Bright.

"Pay him, mother, pay him, and I will tell you
all about it by and by."

"Thirty-five dollars! and all in gold! Where *did*
you get it, Bobby?"

"Never mind it now, mother."

Mr. Hardhand's covetous soul had already grasped
the glittering gold; and removing his hand from the
latch string, he approached the widow.

"I shall be able to pay you forty dollars now," said
Mrs. Bright, taking the five dollars she had saved
from her pocket.

"Yes, marm."

Mr Hardhand took the money, and seating himself at the table, indorsed the amount on the back of the note.

"You owe me sixty more," said he, maliciously, as he returned the note to his pocket book. "It must be paid immediately."

"You must not be hard with me now, when I have paid more than you demanded."

"I don't wish to come here again. That boy's impudence has put me all out of conceit with you and your family," replied Mr. Hardhand, assuming the most benevolent look he could command. "There was a time when I was very willing to help you. I have waited a great while for my pay for this house; a great deal longer than I would have waited for any body else."

"Your interest has always been paid punctually,' suggested the widow, modestly.

"That's true; but very few people would have waited as long as I have for the principal. I wanted to help you ——"

"By gracious!" exclaimed Bobby, interrupting him.

'Don't be saucy, my son, don't," said Mrs. Bright, fearing a repetition of the former scene.

"*He* wanted to help us!" ejaculated Bobby.

It was a very absurd and hypocritical expression on the part of Mr. Hardhand; for he never wanted to help any one but himself; and during the whole period of his relations with the poor widow, he had oppressed, insulted, and abused her to the extent of his capacity, or at least as far as his interest would permit.

He was a malicious and revengeful man. He did not consider the great provocation he had given Bobby for his violent conduct, but determined to be revenged, if it could be accomplished without losing any part of the sixty dollars still due him. He was a wicked man at heart, and would not scruple to turn the widow and her family out of house and home.

Mrs. Bright knew this, and Bobby knew it too; and they felt very uneasy about it. The wretch still had the power to injure them, and he would use it without compunction.

"Yes, young man, I wanted to help you, and you see what I get for it — contempt and insults! You will hear from me again in a day or two. Perhaps you will change your tune, you young reprobate!"

"Perhaps I shall," replied Bobby, without much discretion.

"And you too, marm; you uphold him in his treatment of me. You have not done your duty to him. You have been remiss, marm!" continued Mr. Hardhand, growing bolder again, as he felt the power he wielded.

"That will do, sir; you can go!" said Bobby, springing from his chair, and approaching Mr. Hardhand. "Go, and do your worst!"

"Humph! you stump me — do you?"

"I would rather see my mother kicked out of the house than insulted by such a dried-up old curmudgeon as you are. Go along!"

"Now, don't, Bobby," pleaded his mother.

"I am going; and if the money is not paid by twelve o'clock to-morrow, the law shall take its course;" and Mr. Hardhand rushed out of the house, slamming the door violently after him.

"O Bobby, what have you done?" exclaimed

Mrs. Bright, when the hard-hearted creditor nad departed.

"I could not help it, mother; don't cry. I cannot bear to hear you insulted and abused; and I thought when I heard him do it a year ago, that I couldn't stand it again. It is too bad."

"But he will turn us out of the house; and what shall we do then?"

"Don't cry, mother; it will come round all right. I have friends who are rich and powerful, and who will help us."

"You don't know what you say, Bobby. Sixty dollars is a great deal of money, and if we should sell all we have, it would scarcely bring that."

"Leave it all to me, mother; I feel as though I could do something now. I am old enough to make money."

"What can you do?"

"Now or never!" replied Bobby, whose mind had wandered from the scene to the busy world, where fortunes are made and lost every day. "Now or never!" muttered he again.

"But Bobby, you have not told me where you got all that gold."

"Dinner is ready, I see, and. I will tell you while we eat."

Bobby had been a fishing, and to be hungry is a part of the fisherman's luck; so he seated himself at the table, and gave his mother a full account of all that had occurred at the bridge.

The fond mother trembled when she realized the peril her son had incurred for the sake of the young lady; but her maternal heart swelled with admiration in view of the generous deed, and she thanked God that she was the mother of such a son. She felt more confidence in him then than she had ever felt before, and she realized that he would be the stay and the staff of her declining years.

Bobby finished his dinner, and seated himself on the front door step. His mind was absorbed by a new and brilliant idea; and for half an hour he kept up a most tremendous thinking.

"Now or never!" said he, as he rose and walked down he road towards Riverdale Centre.

CHAPTER V.

IN WHICH BOBBY GIVES HIS NOTE FOR SIXTY DOLLARS.

A GREAT idea was born in Bobby's brain. His mother's weakness and the insecurity of her position were more apparent to him than they had ever been before. She was in the power of her creditor, who might turn her out of the little black house, sell the place at auction, and thus, perhaps, deprive her of the whole or a large part of his father's and her own hard earnings.

But this was not the peculiar hardship of her situation, as her devoted son understood it. It was not the hard work alone which she was called upon to perform, not the coarseness of the fare upon which they lived, not the danger even of being turned out of doors, that distressed Bobby; it was that a wretch like Mr Hardhand could insu't and trample upon hi mother. He had just heard him use language to her that made his blood boil with indignation, and he did not, on cool, sober, second thought, regret that he had taken such a decided stand against it.

He cared not for himself. He could live on a crust of bread and a cup of water from the spring; he could sleep in a barn; he could wear coarse and even ragged clothes; but he could not submit to have his mother insulted, and by such a mean and contemptible person as Mr. Hardhand.

Yet what could he do? He was but a boy, and the great world would look with contempt upon his puny form. But he felt that he was not altogether insignificant. He had performed an act, that day, which the fair young lady,to whom he had rendered the service, had declared very few men would have undertaken. There was something in him, something that would come out, if he only put his best foot forward. It was a tower of strength within him. It told him that he could do wonders; that he could go out into the world and accomplish all that would be required to free his mother from debt, and relieve her from the severe drudgery of her life.

A great many people think they can "do wonders." The vanity of some very silly people makes them think they can command armies, govern nations, and teach the world what the world never knew before, and never would know but for them. But Bobby's something within him was not vanity. It was something more substantial. He was not thinking of becoming a great man, a great general, a great ruler, or a great statesman; not even of making a great fortune. Self was not the idol and the end of his calculations. He was thinking of his mother, and only of her; and the feeling within him was as pure, and holy, and beautiful as the dream of an angel. He wanted to save his mother from insult in the first place, and from a life of ceaseless drudgery in the second.

A legion of angels seemed to have encamped in his soul to give him strength for the great purpose in his mind. His was a holy and a true purpose, and it was this that made him think he could "do wonders."

What Bobby intended to do the reader shall know in due time. It is enough now that he meant to do something. The difficulty with a great many people is, that they never resolve to do something. They wait for "something to turn up;" and as "things" are often very obstinate, they utterly refuse to "turn up" at all. Their lives are spent in waiting for a golden opportunity which never comes.

Now, Bobby Bright repudiated the Micawber philosophy. He would have nothing to do with it. He did not believe corn would grow without being planted, or that pouts would bite the bare hook.

I am not going to tell my young readers now how Bobby made out in the end; but I can confidently say that, if he had waited for "something to turn up," he would have become a vagabond, a loafer, out of money, out at the elbows, and out of patience with himself and all the world.

It was "now or never" with Bobby. He meant to do something; and after he had made up his mind how and where it was to be done, it was no use to stand thinking about it, like the pendulum of the "old clock which had stood for fifty years in a farmer's kitchen, without giving its owner any cause of complaint."

Bobby walked down the road towards the village

with a rapid step. He was thinking very fast, and probably that made him step quick. But as he approached Squire Lee's house, his pace slackened, and he seemed to be very uneasy. When he reached the great gate that led up to the house, he stopped for an instant, and thrust his hands down very deep into his trousers pockets. I cannot tell what the trousers pockets had to do with what he was thinking about; but if he was searching for any thing in them, he did not find it; for after an instant's hesitation he drew out his hands, struck one of them against his chest, and in an audible voice exclaimed,—

"Now or never."

All this pantomime, I suppose, meant that Bobby had some misgivings as to the ultimate success of his mission at Squire Lee's, and that when he struck his breast and uttered his favorite expression, they were conquered and driven out.

Marching with a bold and determined step up to the squire's back door — Bobby's ideas of etiquette would not have answered for the meridian of fashionable society — he gave three smart raps.

Bobby's heart beat a little wildly as he waited a

response to his summons. It seemed that he still had some doubts as to the practicability of his mission; but they were not permitted to disturb him long, for the door was opened by the Squire's pretty daughter Annie, a young miss of twelve.

"O Bobby, is it you? I am so glad you have come!" exclaimed the little lady.

Bobby blushed — he didn't know why, unless it was that the young lady desired to see him. He stammered out a reply, and for the moment forgot the object of his visit.

"I want you to go down to the village for me, and get some books the expressman was to bring up from Boston for me. Will you go?"

"Certainly, Miss Annie, I shall be very glad to go for *you*," replied Bobby with an emphasis that made the little maiden blush in her turn.

"You are real good, Bobby; but I will give you something for going."

"I don't want any thing," said Bobby, stoutly.

"You are too generous! Ah, I heard what you did this forenoon; and pa says that a great many men would not have dared to do what you did. I always thought you were as brave as a lion; now I know it."

"The books are at the express office, I suppose,' said Bobby, turning as red as a blood beet.

"Yes, Bobby; I am so anxious to get them that I can't wait till pa goes down this evening."

"I will not be gone long."

"O, you needn't run, Bobby; take your time."

"I will go very quick. But, Miss Annie, is your father at home?"

"Not now; he has gone over to the wood lot; but he will be back by the time you return."

"Will you please to tell him that I want to see him about something very particular, when he gets back?"

"I will, Bobby."

"Thank you, Miss Annie;" and Bobby hastened to the village to execute his commission.

"I wonder what he wants to see pa so very particularly for," said the young lady to herself, as she watched his receding form. "In my opinion, something has happened at the little black house, for I could see that he looked very sober."

Either Bobby had a very great regard for the young lady, and wished to relieve her impatience to behold the coveted books, or he was in a hurry to see Squire Lee; for the squire's old roan horse could hardly have gone quicker.

"You should not have run, Bobby," said the little maiden when he placed the books in her hand; "I would not have asked you to go if I had thought you would run all the way. You must be very tired."

"Not at all; I didn't run, only walked very quick," replied he; but his quick breathing indicated that his words or his walk had been very much exaggerated. "Has your father returned?"

"He has; he is waiting for you in the sitting room. Come in, Bobby."

Bobby followed her into the room, and took the chair which Annie offered him.

"How do you do, Bobby? I am glad to see you,' said the squire, taking him by the hand, and bestowing a benignant smile upon him — a smile which cheered his heart more than any thing else could at that moment. "I have heard of you before to-day."

"Have you?"

"I have, Bobby; you are a brave little fellow"

"I came over to see you, sir, about something very particular," replied Bobby, whose natural modesty induced him to change the topic.

"Indeed; well, what can I do for you?"

"A great deal, sir; perhaps you will think I am very bold, sir, but I can't help it."

"I know you are a very bold little fellow, or you would not have done what you did this forenoon," laughed the squire.

"I didn't mean that, sir," answered Bobby, blushing up to the eyes.

"I know you didn't; but go on."

"I only meant that you would think me presuming, or impudent, or something of that kind."

"O, no, far from it. You cannot be presuming or impudent. Speak out, Bobby; any thing under the heavens that I can do for you, I shall be glad to do."

"Well, sir, I am going to leave Riverdale."

"Leave Riverdale!"

'Yes, sir; I am going to Boston, where I mean to do something to help mother.'

"Bravo! you are a good lad. What do you mean to do?"

"I was thinking I should go into the book business."

"Indeed!" and Squire Lee was much amused by the matter-of-fact manner of the young aspirant.

"I was talking with a young fellow who went through the place last spring, selling books. He told me that some days he made three or four dollars, and that he averaged twelve dollars a week."

"He did well; perhaps, though, only a few of them make so much."

"I know I can make twelve dollars a week," replied Bobby, confidently, for that something within him made him feel capable of great things.

'I dare say you can. You have energy and perseverance, and people take a liking to you."

"But I wanted to see you about another matter. To speak out at once, I want to borrow sixty dollars of you;" and Bobby blushed, and seemed very much em'.arrassed by his own boldness.

"Sixty dollars!" exclaimed the squire.

"I knew you would think me impudent," replied our hero, his heart sinking within him.

"But I don't, Bobby. You want this money to go
i to business with — to buy your stock of books?"

"O, no, sir; I am going to apply to Mr. Bayard
for that."

"Just so; Mr. Bayard is the gentleman whose
daughter you saved?"

"Yes, sir. I want this money to pay off Mr. Hardhand. We owe him but sixty dollars now, and he has threatened to turn us out, if it is not paid by to-morrow noon."

"The old hunks!"

Bobby briefly related to the squire the events of the morning, much to the indignation and disgust of the honest, kind-hearted man. The courageous boy detailed more clearly his purpose, and doubted not he should be able to pay the loan in a few months.

"Very well, Bobby, here is the money;" and the squire took it from his wallet, and gave it to him.

"Thank you, sir. May Heaven bless you! I shall certainly pay you."

"Don't worry about it, Bobby. Pay it when you get ready."

"I will give you my note, and —— "

The squire laughed heartily at this, and told him, that, as he was a minor, his note was not good for any thing.

"You shall see whether it is, or not," returned Bobby. "Let me give it to you, at least, so that we can tell how much I owe you from time to time."

"You shall have your own way."

Annie Lee, as much amused as her father at Bobby's big talk, got the writing materials, and the little merchant in embryo wrote and signed the note.

"Good, Bobby! Now promise that you will come and see me every time you come home, and tell me how you are getting along."

"I will, sir, with the greatest pleasure;" and with a light heart Bobby tripped away home.

CHAPTER VI.

IN WHICH BOBBY SETS OUT ON HIS TRAVELS.

SQUIRE LEE, though only a plain farmer, was the richest man in Riverdale. He had taken a great fancy to Bobby, and often employed him to do errands, ride the horse to plough in the cornfields, and such chores about the place as a boy could do. He liked to talk with Bobby because there was a great deal of good sense in him, for one with a small head.

If there was any one thing upon which the squire particularly prided himself, it was his knowledge of human nature. He declared that he only wanted to look a man in the face to know what he was; and as for Bobby Bright, he had summered him and wintered him, and he was satisfied that he would make something in good time.

He was not much astonished when Bobby opened his ambitious scheme of going into business for himself. B. he had full faith in his ability to work out a useful and profitable, if not a brilliant life. He often said that Bobby was worth his weight in gold, and that he would trust him with any thing he had. Perhaps he did not suspect that the time was at hand when he would be called upon to verify his words practically; for it was only that morning, when one of the neighbors told him about Bobby's stopping the horse, that he had repeated the expression for the twentieth time.

It was not an idle remark. Sixty dollars was hardly worth mentioning with a man of his wealth and liberal views, though so careful a man as he was would not have been likely to throw away that amount. But as a matter of investment,—Bobby had made the note read "with interest,"—he would as readily have let him have it, as the next richest man in the place, so much confidence had he in our hero's integrity, and so sure was he that he would soon have the means of paying him.

Bobby was overjoyed at the fortunate issue of his mission, and he walked into the room where his mother was closing shoes, with a dignity worthy a

banker or a great merchant. Mrs. Bright was very
sad. Perhaps she felt a little grieved that her son
whom she loved so much, had so thoughtlessly
plunged her into a new difficulty.

"Come, cheer up, mother; it is all right," said
Bobby in his usual elastic and gay tones; and at the
same time he took the sixty dollars from his pocket
and handed it to her. "There is the money, and
you will be forever quit of Mr. Hardhand to morrow"

"What, Bobby! Why, where did you get all this
money?" asked Mrs. Bright, utterly astonished.

In a few words the ambitious boy told his story,
and then informed his mother that he was going to
Boston the next Monday morning, to commence business for himself.

"Why, what can you do, Bobby?"

"Do? I can do a great many things;' and he
unfolded his scheme of becoming a little book merchant.

"You are a courageous fellow! Who would have
thought of such a thing?"

"I should, and did."

"But you are not old enough."

"O, yes, I am."

"You had better wait a while."

"Now or never, mother! You see I have given my note, and my paper will be dishonored, if I am not up and doing."

"Your paper!" said Mrs. Bright, with a smile.

"That is what Mr. Wing, the boot manufacturer, calls it."

"You needn't go away to earn this money; I can pay it myself."

"This note is my affair, and I mean to pay it myself with my own earnings. No objections, mother."

Like a sensible woman as she was, she did not make any objections. She was conscious of Bobby's talents; she knew that he had a strong mind of his own, and could take care of himself. It is true, she feared the influence of the great world, and especially of the great city, upon the tender mind of her son; but if he was never tempted, he would never be a conqueror over the foes that beset him.

She determined to do her whole duty towards him; and she carefully pointed out to him the sins and the moral danger to which he would be exposed, and warned him always to resist temptation. She counselled him to think of her when he felt like going astray.

Bobby declared that he would try to be a good boy. He did not speak contemptuously of the anticipated perils, as many boys would have done, because he knew that his mother would not make bugbears out of things which she knew had no real existence.

The next day, Mr. Hardhand came; and my young readers can judge how astonished and chagrined he was, when the widow Bright offered him the sixty dollars. The Lord was with the widow and the fatherless, and the wretch was cheated out of his revenge. The note was given up, and the mortgage cancelled.

Mr. Hardhand insisted that she should pay the interest on the sixty dollars for one day, as it was then the second day of July; but when Bobby reckoned it up, and found it was less than one cent, even the wretched miser seemed ashamed of himself, and changed the subject of conversation.

He did not dare to say any thing saucy to the

widow this time. He had lost his power over her and there stood Bobby, who had come to look just like a young lion to him, coward and knave as he was.

The business was all settled now, and Bobby spent the rest of the week in getting ready for his great enterprise. He visited all his friends, and went each day to talk with Squire Lee and Annie. The little maiden promised to buy a great many books of him, if he would bring his stock to Riverdale, for she was quite as much interested in him as her father was.

Monday morning came, and Bobby was out of bed with the first streak of dawn. The excitement of the great event which was about to happen had not permitted him to sleep for the two hours preceding; yet when he got up, he could not help feeling sad. He was going to leave the little black house, going to leave his mother, going to leave the children, to depart for the great city.

His mother was up before him. She was even more sad than he was, for she could see plainer than he the perils that environed him, and her maternal heart, in spite of the reasonable confidence she had in his integrity and good principles, trembled for his safety.

As he ate his breakfast, his mother repeated the warnings and the good lessons she had before imparted. She particularly cautioned him to keep out of bad company. If he found that his companions would lie and swear, he might depend upon it they would steal, and he had better forsake them at once. This was excellent advice, and Bobby had occasion at a later period to call it to his sorrowing heart.

"Here is three dollars, Bobby; it is all the money I have. Your fare to Boston will be one dollar, and you will have two left to pay the expenses of your first trip. It is all I have now," said Mrs. Bright.

"I will not take the whole of it. You will want it yourself. One dollar is enough. When I find Mr. Bayard, I shall do very well."

"Yes, Bobby, take the whole of it."

"I will take just one dollar, and no more," replied Bobby, resolutely, as he handed her the other two dollars.

"Do take it, Bobby."

"No, mother; it will only make me lazy and indifferent."

Taking a clean shirt, a pair of socks, and a handkerchief in his bundle, he was ready for a start.

"Good by, mother," said he, kissing her and taking her hand. "I shall try and come home on Saturday, so as to be with you on Sunday."

Then kissing the children, who had not yet got up, and to whom he had bidden adieu the night before, he left the house. He had seen the flood of tears that filled his mother's eyes, as he crossed the threshold; and he could not help crying a little himself. It is a sad thing to leave one's home, one's mother, especially, to go out into the great world; and we need not wonder that Bobby, who had hardly been out of Riverdale before, should weep. But he soon restrained the flowing tears.

"Now or never!" said he, and he put his best foot forward.

It was an epoch in his history, and though he was too young to realize the importance of the event, he seemed to feel that what he did now was to give character to his whole future life.

It was a bright and beautiful morning — somehow, t is always a bright and beautiful morning when boys leave their homes to commence the journey of life ; it is typical of the season of youth and hope, and it is meet that the sky should be clear, and the sun shine brightly, when the little pilgrim sets out upon his tour. He will see clouds and storms before he has gone far — let him have a fair start.

He had to walk five miles to the nearest railroad station. His road lay by the house of his friend, Squire Lee; and as he was approaching it, he met Annie. She said she had come out to take her morning walk; but Bobby knew very well that she did not usually walk till an hour later; which, with the fact that she had asked him particularly, the day before, what time he was going, made Bobby believe that she had come out to say good by, and bid him God speed on his journey. At any rate, he was very glad to see her. He said a great many pretty things to her, and talked so big about what he was going to do, that the little maiden could hardly help laughing in his face.

Then at the house he shook hands with the squire

nd shook hands again with Annie, and resumed his journey. His heart felt lighter for having met them, or at least for having met one of them, if not both; for Annie's eyes were so full of sunshine that they seemed to gladden his heart, and make him feel truer and stronger.

After a pleasant walk, for he scarcely heeded the distance, so full was he of his big thoughts, he reached the railroad station. The cars had not yet arrived, and would not for half an hour.

" Why should I give them a dollar for carrying me to Boston, when I can just as well walk? If I get tired, I can sit down and rest me. If I save the dollar, I shall have to earn only fifty-nine more to pay my note. So here goes;" and he started down the track.

CHAPTER VII.

IN WHICH BOBBY STANDS UP FOR "CERTAIN IN-
ALIENABLE RIGHTS."

WHETHER it was wise policy, or "penny wise and pound foolish" policy for Bobby to undertake such a long walk, is certainly a debatable question; but as my young readers would probably object to an argument, we will follow him to the city, and let every one settle the point to suit himself.

His cheerful heart made the road smooth beneath his feet. He had always been accustomed to an active, busy life, and had probably often walked more than twenty miles in a day. About ten o'clock, though he did not feel much fatigued, he seated himself on a rock by a brook from which he had just taken a drink, to rest himself. He had walked slowly so as to husband his strength; and he felt confident that he should be able to accomplish the journey without injury to himself.

After resting for half an hour, he resumed his walk At twelve o'clock he reached a point from which he obtained his first view of the city. His heart bounded at the sight, and his first impulse was to increase his speed so that he should the sooner gratify his curiosity; but a second thought reminded him that he had eaten nothing since breakfast; so, finding a shady tree by the road side, he seated himself on a stone to eat the luncheon which his considerate mother had placed in his bundle.

Thus refreshed, he felt like a new man, and continued his journey again till he was on the very outskirts of the city, where a sign, " No passing over this bridge," interrupted his farther progress. Unlike many others, Bobby took this sign literally, and did not venture to cross the bridge. Having some doubts as to the direct road to the city, he hailed a man in a butcher's cart, who not only pointed the way, but gave him an invitation to ride with him, which Bobby was glad to accept.

They crossed the Milldam, and the little pilgrim forgot the long walk he had taken — forgot Riverdale, his mother, Squire Lee, and Annie, for the time, in the absorbing interest of the exciting scene. The Common beat Riverdale Common all hollow; he had never seen any thing like it before. But when the wagon reached Washington Street, the measure of his surprise was filled up.

"My gracious! how thick the houses are!" exclaimed he, much to the amusement of the kind-hearted butcher.

"We have high fences here," he replied.

"Where are all these folks going to?"

"You will have to ask them, if you want to know."

But the wonder soon abated, and Bobby began to think of his great mission in the city. He got tired of gazing and wondering, and even began to smile with contempt at the silly fops as they sauntered along, and the gayly-dressed ladies, that flaunted like so many idle butterflies, on the sidewalk. It was an exciting scene; but it did not look real to him. It was more like Herr Grunderslung's exhibition of the magic lantern, than any thing substantial. The men and women were like so many puppets. They did not seem to be doing any thing, or to be walking for any purpose.

He got out of the butcher's cart at the Old South. His first impression, as he joined the busy throng, was, that he was one of the puppets. He did not seem to have any hold upon the scene, and for several minutes this sensation of vacancy chained him to the spot.

"All right!" exclaimed he to himself at last. "I am here. Now's my time to make a strike. Now or never."

He pulled Mr. Bayard's card from his pocket, and fixed the number of his store in his mind. Now, numbers were not a Riverdale institution, and Bobby was a little perplexed about finding the one indicated. A little study into the matter, however, set him right, and he soon had the satisfaction of seeing the bookseller's name over his store.

"F. Bayard," he read; "this is the place."

"Country!" shouted a little ragged boy, who dodged across the street at that moment.

"Just so, my beauty!" said Bobby, a little nettled at this imputation of verdancy.

"What a greeny!" shouted the little vagabond from the other side of the street.

"No matter, rag-tag! We'll settle that matter some other time."

But Bobby felt that there was something in his appearance which subjected him to the remarks of others, and as he entered the shop, he determined to correct it as soon as possible.

A spruce young gentleman was behind the counter, who cast a mischievous glance at him as he entered.

"Mr. Bayard keep here?" asked Bobby.

"Well, I reckon he does. How are all the folks up country?" replied the spruce clerk, with a rude grin.

"How are they?" repeated Bobby, the color flying to his cheek.

"Yes, ha-ow do they dew?"

"They behave themselves better than they do here."

"Eh, greeny?"

"Eh, sappy?" repeated Bobby, mimicking the soft, silky tones of the young city gentleman.

"What do you mean by sappy?" asked the clerk, indignantly.

"What do you mean by greeny?"

"I'll let you know what I mean!"

"When you do, I'll let you know what I mean by sappy."

"Good!" exclaimed one of the salesmen, who had heard part of this spirited conversation. "You will learn better by and by, Timmins, than to impose upon boys from out of town."

"You seem to be a gentleman, sir," said Bobby, approaching the salesman. "I wish to see Mr. Bayard."

"You can't see him!" growled Timmins.

"Can't I?"

"Not at this minute; he is engaged just now," added the salesman, who seemed to have a profound respect for Bobby's discrimination. "He will be at liberty in a few moments."

"I will wait, then," said Bobby, seating himself on a stool by the counter.

Pretty soon the civil gentleman left the store to go to dinner, and Timmins, a little timid about provoking the young lion, cast an occasional glance of hatred at him. He had evidently found that "Country" was an embryo American citizen, and that he was a firm believer in the self-evident truths of the Declaration of Independence.

Bobby bore no ill will towards the spruce clerk ready as he had been to defend his "certain inalienable rights."

"You do a big business here," suggested Bobby, in a conciliatory tone, and with a smile on his face which ought to have convinced the uncourteous clerk that he meant well.

"Who told you so?" replied Timmins, gruffly.

"I merely judged from appearances. You have a big store, and an immense quantity of books."

"Appearances are deceitful," replied Timmins; and perhaps he had been impressed by the fact from his experience with the lad from the country.

"That is true," added Bobby, with a good-natured smile, which, when interpreted, might have meant, " I took you for a civil fellow, but I have been very much mistaken."

"You will find it out before you are many days older."

"The book business is good just now, isn't it?" continued Bobby, without clearly comprehending the meaning of the other's last remark.

"Humph! What's that to you?"

"O, I intend to go into it myself."

"Ha, ha, ha! Good! You do?"

"I do," replied Bobby, seemingly unconcerned at the taunts of the clerk.

"I suppose you want to get a place here," sneered Timmins, alarmed at the prospect. "But let me tell you, you can't do it. Bayard has all the help he wants; and if that is what you come for, you can move on as fast as you please."

"I guess I will see him," added Bobby quietly.

"No use."

"No harm in seeing him."

As he spoke he took up a book that lay on the counter, and began to turn over the leaves.

"Put that book down!" said the amiable Mr. Timmins.

"I won't hurt it," replied Bobby, who had just fixed his eye upon some very pretty engravings in the volume.

"Put it down!" repeated Mr. Timmins, in a loud imperative tone.

"Certainly I will, if you say so," said Bobby, who

though not much intimidated by the harsh tones of the clerk, did not know the rules of the store, and deemed it prudent not to meddle.

"I *do* say so!" added Mr. Timmins, magnificently; "and what's more, you'd better mind me, too."

Bobby had minded, and probably the stately little clerk would not have been so bold if he had not. Some people like to threaten after the danger is over.

Then our visitor from the country espied some little blank books lying on the counter. He had already made up his mind to have one, in which to keep his accounts; and he thought, while he was waiting, that he would purchase one. He meant to do things methodically; so when he picked up one of the blank books, it was with the intention of buying it.

"Put that book down!" said Mr. Timmins, encouraged in his aggressive intentions by the previous docility of our hero.

"I want to buy one."

"No, you don't: put it down."

"What is the price of these?" asked Bobby, resolutely.

"None of your business!"

"Is that the way you treat your customers?" asked Bobby, with a little sternness in his looks and tones. "I say I want to buy one."

"Put it down!"

"But I will not; I say I want to buy it."

"No, you don't!"

"What is the price of it?"

"Twenty-five cents," growled Timmins, which was just four times the retail price.

"Twenty-five cents! That's high."

"Put it down, then."

"Is that your lowest price?" asked Bobby, who was as cool as a cucumber.

"Yes, it is; and if you don't put it down, I'll kick you out of the store."

"Will you? Then I won't put it down."

Mr. Timmins took this as a "stump;" his ire was up, and he walked round from behind the counter to execute his threat.

I must say I think Bobby was a little forward, and I would have my young readers a little more pliant with small men like Timmins. There are always men enough in the world who are ready and willing to quarrel on any provocation; and it is always best not to provoke them, even if they are overbearing and insolent, as Mr. Timmins certainly was.

"Hold on a minute before you do it," said Bobby, with the same provoking coolness. "I want to buy this book, and I am willing to pay a fair price for it. But I happen to know that you can buy them up in Riverdale, where I came from, for six cents."

"No matter," exclaimed the indignant clerk, seizing Bobby by the coat collar for the purpose of ejecting him; "you shall find your way into the street."

Now, Bobby, as I have before intimated, was an embryo American citizen, and the act of Mr. Timmins seemed like an invasion of his inalienable rights. No time was given him to make a formal declaration of rights in the premises; so the instinct of self-preservation was allowed to have free course.

Mr. Timmins pulled and tugged at his coat collar, and Bobby hung back like a mule; and for an instant there was quite a spirited scene.

"Hallo! Timmins, what does this mean?" said a voice, at which the valiant little clerk instantly let go his hold.

CHAPTER VIII.

IN WHICH MR. TIMMINS IS ASTONISHED, AND BOBBY DINES IN CHESTNUT STREET.

It was Mr. Bayard. He had finished his business with the gentleman by his side, and hearing the noise of the scuffle, had come to learn the occasion of it.

"This impudent young puppy wouldn't let the books alone!" began Mr. Timmins. "I threatened to turn him out if he didn't; and I meant to make good my threat. I think he meant to steal something."

Bobby was astonished and shocked at this bold imputation; but he wished to have his case judged on its own merits; so he turned his face away, that Mr. Bayard might not recognize him.

"I wanted to buy one of these blank books," added Bobby, picking up the one he had dropped on the or in the struggle.

"All stuff!" ejaculated Timmins. "He is an impudent, obstinate puppy! In my opinion he meant to steal that book."

"I asked him the price, and told him I wanted to buy it," added Bobby, still averting his face.

"Well, I told him; and he said it was too high."

"He asked me twenty-five cents for it."

"Is this true, Timmins?" asked Mr. Bayard, sternly.

"No, *sir!* I told him fourpence," replied Timmins boldly.

"By gracious! What a whopper!" exclaimed Bobby, startled out of his propriety by this monstrous lie. "He said twenty-five cents; and I told him I could buy one up in Riverdale, where I came from, for six cents. Can you deny that?"

"It's a lie!" protested Timmins.

"Riverdale," said Mr. Bayard. "Are you from Riverdale, boy?"

"Yes, sir, I am; and if you will look on your memorandum book you will find my name there."

"Bless me! I am sure I have seen that face before," exclaimed Mr. Bayard, as he grasped the hand of

Bobby, much to the astonishment and consternation of Mr. Timmins. You are ——"

"Robert Bright, sir."

"My brave little fellow! I am heartily glad to see you;" and the bookseller shook the hand he held with hearty good will. "I was thinking of you only a little while ago."

"This fellow calls me a liar," said Bobby, pointing to the astonished Mr. Timmins, who did not know what to make of the cordial reception which "Country" was receiving from his employer.

"Well, Robert, we know that *he* is a liar; this is not the first time he has been caught in a lie. Timmins, your time is out."

The spruce clerk hung his head with shame and mortification.

"I hope, sir, you will ——" he began, but pride or fear stopped him short.

"Don't be hard with him, sir, if you please," said Bobby. "I suppose I aggravated him."

Mr. Bayard looked at the gentleman who stood by his side, and a smile of approbation lighted up his face.

"Generous as he is noble! Butler, this is the boy that saved Ellen."

"Indeed! He is a little giant!" replied Mr Butler, grasping Bobby's hand.

Even Timmins glanced with something like admiration in his looks at the youth whom he had so lately despised. Perhaps, too, he thought of that Scripture wisdom about entertaining angels unawares. He was very much abashed, and nothing but his silly pride prevented him from acknowledging his error and begging Bobby's forgiveness.

"I can't have a liar about me," said Mr. Bayard.

"There may be some mistake," suggested Mr Butler.

"I think not. Robert Bright couldn't lie. So brave and noble a boy is incapable of a falsehood. Besides, I got a letter from my friend Squire Lee by this morning's mail, in which he informed me of my young friend's coming."

Mr. Bayard took from his pocket a bundle of letters, and selected the squire's from among them. Opening it, he read a passage which had a direct bearing upon the case before him.

"'I do not know what Bobby's faults are,'"—the letter said,—"'but this I do know: that Bobby would rather be whipped than tell a lie. He is noted through the place for his love of truth.'—That is pretty strong testimony; and you see, Bobby,—tnat's what the squire calls you,—your reputation has preceded you."

Bobby blushed, as he always did when he was praised, and Mr. Timmins was more abashed than ever.

"Did you hear that, Timmins? Who is the liar now?" said Mr. Bayard, turning to the culprit.

"Forgive me, sir, this time. If you turn me off now, I cannot get another place, and my mother depends upon my wages."

"You ought to have thought of this before."

"He aggravated me, sir, so that I wanted to pay him off."

"As to that, he commenced upon me the moment I came into the store. But don't turn him off, if you please, sir," said Bobby, who even now wished no harm to his discomfited assailant. "He will do better hereafter: won't you, Timmins?"

Thus appealed to, Timmins, though he did not relish so direct an inquiry, and from such a source, was compelled to reply in the affirmative; and Mr. Bayard graciously remitted the sentence he had passed against the offending clerk.

"Now, Robert, you will come over to my house and dine with me. Ellen will be delighted to see you."

"Thank you, sir," replied Bobby, bashfully, "I have been to dinner" — referring to the luncheon he had eaten at Brighton.

"But you must go to the house with me."

"I should be very glad to do so, sir, but I came on business. I will stay here with Mr. Timmins till you come back."

The truth is, he had heard something about the fine houses of the city, and how stylish the people were, and he had some misgivings about venturing into such a strange and untried scene as the parlor of a Boston merchant.

"Indeed, you must come with me. Ellen would never forgive you or me, if you do not come."

"I would rather rest here till you return," replied

Bobby, still willing to escape the fire house and the fine folks. "I walked from Riverdale, sir, and I am rather tired."

"Walked!" exclaimed Mr. Bayard. "Had you no money?"

"Yes, sir, enough to pay my passage; but Dr. Franklin says that 'a penny saved is a penny earned,' and I thought I would try it. I shall get rested by the time you return."

"But you must go with me. Timmins, go and get a carriage."

Timmins obeyed, and before Mr. Bayard had finished asking Bobby how all the people in Riverdale were, the carriage was at the door.

There was no backing out now, and our hero was obliged to get into the vehicle, though it seemed altogether too fine for a poor boy like him. Mr. Bayard and Mr. Butler (whom the former had invited to dine with him) seated themselves beside him, and the driver was directed to set them down at No. —, Chestnut Street, where they soon arrived.

Though my readers would, no doubt, be very much amused to learn how carefully Bobby trod the velvet carpets, how he stared with wonder at the drapery curtains, at the tall mirrors, the elegant chandeliers, and the fantastically shaped chairs and tables that adorned Mr. Bayard's parlor, the length of our story does not permit us to pause over these trivial matters.

When Ellen Bayard was informed that her little deliverer was in the house, she rushed into the parlor like a hoiden school girl, grasped both his hands, kissed both his rosy cheeks, and behaved just as though she had never been to a boarding school in her life.

She had thought a great deal about Bobby since that eventful day, and the more she thought of him, the more she liked him. Her admiration of him was not of that silly, sentimental character which moonstruck young ladies cherish towards those immaculate young men who have saved them from drowning in a horse pond, pulled them back just as they were tumbling over a precipice two thousand five hundred feet high, or rescued them from a house seven stories high, bearing them down a ladder seventy-five odd feet long. The fact was, Bobby was a boy of thirteen and there was no chance for much sentiment; so the young lady's regard was real, earnest, and lifelike.

Ellen said a great many very handsome things; bu I am sure she never thought of such a thing as that he would run away with her, in case her papa was unnecessarily obstinate. She was very glad to see him, and I have no doubt she wished Bobby might be her brother, it would be so glorious to have such a noble little fellow always with her.

Bobby managed the dinner much better than he had anticipated; for Mr. Bayard insisted that he snould sit down with them, whether he ate any thing or not. But the Rubicon passed, our hero found that he had a pretty smart appetite, and did full justice to the viands set before him. Is is true the silver forks, the napkins, the finger bowls, and other articles of luxury and show, to which he had been entirely unaccustomed, bothered him not a little; but he kept perfectly cool, and carefully observed how Mr. Butler, who sat next to him, handled the " spoon fork," what ne did with the napkin and the finger bowl, so that, I will venture to say, not one in ten would have suspected he had not spent his life in the parlor of a *millionnaire*.

Dinner over, the party returned to the parlor, where Bobby unfolded his plan for the future. To make his story intelligible, he was obliged to tell them all about Mr. Hardhand.

"The old wretch!" exclaimed Mr. Bayard. "But, Robert, you must let me advance the sixty dollars, to pay Squire Lee."

"No, sir; you have done enough in that way. I have given my note for the money."

"Whew!" said Mr. Butler.

"And I shall soon earn enough to pay it."

"No doubt of it. You are a lad of courage and energy, and you will succeed in every thing you undertake."

"I shall want you to trust me for a stock of books on the strength of old acquaintance," continued Bobby, who had now grown quite bold, and felt as much at home in the midst of the costly furniture, as he did in the "living room" of the old black house.

"You shall have all the books you want."

"I will pay for them as soon as I return. The truth is, Mr. Bayard, I mean to be independent. I didn't want to take that thirty-five dollars, though I den't know what Mr. Hardhand would have done to us, if I hadn't."

"Ellen said I ought to have given you a hundred, and I think so myself."

"I am glad you didn't. Too much money makes us fat and lazy."

Mr. Bayard laughed at the easy self-possession of the lad — at his big talk; though, big as it was, it meant something. When he proposed to go to the store, he told Bobby he had better stay at the house and rest himself.

"No, sir; I want to start out to-morrow, and I must get ready to-day."

"You had better put it off till the next day; you will feel more like it then."

"Now or never," replied Bobby. "That is my motto, sir. If we have any thing to do, now is always the best time to do it. Dr. Franklin says, 'Never put off till to-morrow what you can do to day.'"

"Right, Robert! you shall have your own way I wish my clerks would adopt some of Dr. Franklin's wise saws. I should be a great deal better off in the course of a year if they would."

CHAPTER IX.

IN WHICH BOBBY OPENS VARIOUS ACCOUNTS, AND WINS HIS FIRST VICTORY.

" Now, Bobby, I understand your plan," said Mr. Bayard, when they reached the store; " but the details must be settled. Where do you intend to go?"

" I hardly know, sir. I suppose I can sell books almost any where."

" Very true; but in some places much better than in others."

Mr. Bayard mentioned a large town about eighteen miles from the city, in which he thought a good trade might be carried on, and Bobby at once decided to adopt the suggestion.

" You can make this place your head quarters for the week; if books do not sell well right in tne village, why, you can go out a little way, for the country in the vicinity is peopled by intelligent farmers, who are well off, and who can afford to buy books."

"I was thinking of that; but what shall I take with me, sir?"

"There is a new book just published, called 'The Wayfarer,' which is going to have a tremendous run. It has been advertised in advance all over the country, so that you will find a ready sale for it. You will get it there before any one else, and have the market all to yourself."

"The Wayfarer? I have heard of it myself."

"You shall take fifty copies with you, and if you find that you shall want more, write, and I will send them."

"But I cannot carry fifty copies."

"You must take the cars to B———, and have a trunk or box to carry your books in. I have a stout trunk down cellar which you shall have."

"I will pay for it, sir."

"Never mind that, Bobby; and you will want a small valise or carpet bag to carry your books from house to house. I will lend you one."

"You are very kind, sir; I did not mean to ask

any favors of you except to trust me for the books until my return."

"All right, Bobby."

Mr. Bayard called the porter and ordered him to bring up the trunk, in which he directed Mr. Timmins to pack fifty "Wayfarers."

"Now, how much will these books cost me apiece?" asked Bobby.

"The retail price is one dollar; the wholesale price is one third off; and you shall have them at what they cost me."

"Sixty-seven cents," added Bobby. "That will give me a profit of thirty-three cents on each book."

"Just so."

"Perhaps Mr. Timmins will sell me one of those blank books now; for I like to have things down in black and white."

"I will furnish you with something much better than that;" and Mr. Bayard left the counting room.

In a moment he returned with a handsome pocket memorandum book, which he presented to the little merchant.

"But I don't like to take it unless you will let m. pay for it," said Bobby, hesitating.

"Never mind it, my young friend. Now you can sit down at my desk and open your accounts. I like to see boys methodical, and there is nothing like keeping accounts to make one accurate. Keep your books posted up, and you will know where you are at any time."

"I intend to keep an account of all I spend and all I receive, if it is no more than a cent."

"Right, my little man. Have you ever studied book-keeping?"

"No, sir, I suppose I haven't; but there was a page of accounts in the back part of the arithmetic I studied, and I got a pretty good idea of the thing from that. All the money received goes on one side, and all the money paid out goes on the other."

"Exactly so; in this book you had better open a book account first. If you wish, I will show you how."

"Thank you, sir; I should be very glad to have you;" and Bobby opened the memorandum book, and seated himself at the desk.

"Write 'Book Account,' at the top of the pages

one word on each. Very well. Now write 'To fifty copies of Wayfarer, at sixty-seven cents, $33.50,' on the left hand page, or debit side of the account."

"I am not much of a writer," said Bobby, apologetically.

"You will improve. Now, each day you will credit the amount of sales on the right hand page, or credit side of the account; so, when you have sold out, the balance due your debit side will be the profit on the lot. Do you understand it?"

Bobby thought a moment before he could see through it; but his brain was active, and he soon managed the idea.

"Now you want a personal account;" and Mr. Bayard explained to him how to make this out.

He then instructed him to enter on the debit side all he spent for travel, board, freight, and other charges. The next was the "profit and loss" account, which was to show him the net profit of the business.

Our hero, who had a decided taste for accounts, was very much pleased with this employment; and when the accounts were all opened, he regarded them with a great deal of satisfaction. He longed to commence his operations, if it were only for the pleasure of making the entries in this book.

"One thing I forgot," said he, as he seized the pen, and under the cash account entered, "To Cash from mother, $1.00." "Now I am all right, I believe."

"I think you are. Now, the cars leave at seven in the morning. Can you be ready for a start as early as that?" asked Mr. Bayard.

"O, yes, sir, I hope so. I get up at half past four at home."

"Very well; my small valise is at the house; but I believe every thing else is ready. Now, I have some business to attend to; and if you will amuse yourself for an hour or two, we will go home then."

"I shall want a lodging place when I am in the city; perhaps some of your folks can direct me to one where they won't charge too much."

"As to that, Bobby, you must go to my house whenever you are in the city."

"Law, sir! you live so grand, I couldn't think of going to your house. I am only a poor boy from the country, and I don't know how to behave myself among such nice folks."

"You will do very well, Bobby. Ellen would never forgive me if I let you go any where else. So that is settled; you will go to my house. Now, you may sit here, or walk out and see the sights."

"If you please, sir, if Mr. Timmins will let me look at some of the books, I shouldn't wish for any thing better. I should like to look at the Wayfarer, so that I shall know how to recommend it."

"Mr. Timmins *will* let you," replied Mr. Bayard, as he touched the spring of a bell on his desk.

The dapper clerk came running into the counting-room to attend the summons of his employer.

"Mr. Timmins," continued Mr. Bayard, with a mischievous smile, "bring Mr. Bright a copy of 'The Wayfarer.'"

Mr. Timmins was astonished to hear "Country" called "Mister," astonished to hear his employer call him "Mister," and Bobby was astonished to hear himself called "Mister;" nevertheless, our hero enjoyed the joke.

The clerk brought the book; and Bobby proceeded to give it a thorough, critical examination. He read the
nd several chapters

"How do you like it, Bobby?" asked the bookseller.

"First rate."

"You may take that copy in your hand; you will want to finish it."

"Thank you, sir; I will be careful of it."

"You may keep it. Let that be the beginning of your own private library."

His own private library! Bobby had not got far enough to dream of such a thing yet; but he thanked Mr. Bayard, and put the book under his arm.

After tea, Ellen proposed to her father that they should all go to the Museum. Mr. Bayard acceded, and our hero was duly amazed at the drolleries perpetrated there. He had a good time; but it was so late when he went to bed, that he was a little fearful lest he should oversleep himself in the morning.

He did not, however, and was down in the parlor before any of the rest of the family were stirring. An early breakfast was prepared for him, at which Mr. Bayard, who intended to see him off, joined him. Depositing his little bundle and the copy of "The Wayfarer" in the valise provided for him, they walked to the store. The porter wheeled the trunk down to the railroad station, though Bobby insisted upon doing it himself.

The bookseller saw him and his baggage safely aboard of the cars, gave him a ticket, and then bade him an affectionate adieu. In a little while Bobby was flying over the rail, and at about eight o'clock reached B——.

The station master kindly permitted him to deposit his trunk in the baggage room, and to leave it there for the remainder of the week.

Taking a dozen of the books from the trunk, and placing them in his valise, he sallied out upon his mission. It must be confessed that his heart was filled with a tumult of emotions. The battle of life was before him. He was on the field, sword in hand, ready to plunge into the contest. It was victory or defeat.

"March on, brave youth! the field of strife
With peril fraught before thee lies;
March on! the battle plain of life
Shall yield thee yet a glorious prize"

It was of no use to shrink then, even if he had felt

disposed to do so. He was prepared to be rebuffed, to be insulted, to be turned away from the doors at which he should seek admission; but he was determined to conquer.

He had reached a house at which he proposed to offer " The Wayfarer" for sale. His heart went pit pat, pit pat, and he paused before the door.

"Now or never!" exclaimed he, as he swung open the garden gate, and made his way up to the door.

He felt some misgivings. It was so new and strange to him that he could hardly muster sufficient resolution to proceed farther. But his irresolution was of only a moment's duration.

"Now or never!" and he gave a vigorous knock at the door.

It was opened by an elderly lady, whose physiognomy did not promise much.

" Good morning, ma'am. Can I sell you a copy of ' The Wayfarer to-day? a new book, just published."

"No; I don't want none of your books. There's more pedlers round the country now than you could shake a stick at in a month," replied the old lady petulantly

"It is a very interesting book, ma'am; has an excellent moral." Bobby had read the preface, as I before remarked. "It will suit you, ma'am; for you look just like a lady who wants to read something with a moral."

Bravo, Bobby! The lady concluded that her face had a moral expression, and she was pleased with the idea.

"Let me see it;" and she asked Bobby to walk in and be seated, while she went for her spectacles.

As she was looking over the book, our hero went into a more elaborate recommendation of its merits. He was sure it would interest the young and the old; it taught a good lesson; it had elegant engravings; the type was large, which would suit her eyes; it was well printed and bound; and finally, it was cheap at one dollar.

"I'll take it," said the old lady.

"Thank you, ma'am."

Bobby's first victory was achieved

"Have you got a dollar?" asked the lady, as she handed him a two dollar bill.

"Yes, ma'am;" and he gave her his only dollar

and put the two in its place, prouder than a king who has conquered an empire. "Thank you, ma'am."

Bidding the lady a polite good morning, he left the house, encouraged by his success to go forward in his mission with undiminished hope.

CHAPTER X.

IN WHICH BOBBY IS A LITTLE TOO SMART.

THE clouds were rolled back, and Bobby no longe had a doubt as to the success of his undertaking. I, requires but a little sunshine to gladden the heart, and the influence of his first success scattered all the misgivings he had cherished.

Two New England shillings is undoubtedly a very small sum of money; but Bobby had made two shillings, and he would not have considered himself more fortunate if some unknown relative had left him a fortune. It gave him confidence in his powers, and as he walked away from the house, he reviewed the circumstances of his first sale.

The old lady had told him at first she did not wish to buy a book, and, moreover, had spoken rather contemptuously of the craft to which he had now the honor to belong. H; gave himself the credit of having conquered the old lady's prejudices. He had sold her a book in spite of her evident intention not to purchase. In short, he had, as we have before said, won a glorious victory, and he congratulated himself accordingly.

But it was of no use to waste time in useless self-glorification, and Bobby turned from the past to the future. There were forty-nine more books to be sold; so that the future was forty-nine times as big as the past.

He saw a shoemaker's shop ahead of him; and he was debating with himself whether he should enter and offer his books for sale. It would do no harm, though he had but slight expectations of doing any thing.

There were three men at work in the shop — one of them a middle-aged man, the other two young men. They looked like persons of intelligence, and as soon as Bobby saw them his hopes grew stronger.

"Can I sell you any books to-day?" asked the little merchant, as he crossed the threshold.

"Well, I don't know; that depends upon how smart you are," replied the eldest of the men. "It takes a pretty smart fellow to sell any thing in this shop."

"Then I hope to sell each of you a book," added Bobby, laughing at the badinage of the shoemaker.

Opening his valise he took out three copies of his book, and politely handed one to each of the men.

"It isn't every book pedler that comes along who offers you such a work as that. 'The Wayfarer' is decidedly *the* book of the season."

"You don't say so!" said the oldest shoemaker, with a laugh. "Every pedler that comes along uses those words, precisely."

"Do they? They steal my thunder then."

"You are an old one."

"Only thirteen. I was born where they don't fasten the door with a boiled carrot."

"What do they fasten them with?"

"They don't fasten them at all."

"There are no book pedlers round there, then;' and all the shoemakers laughed heartily at this smart sally.

"No; they are all shoemakers in our town."

"You can take my hat, boy."

"You will want it to put your head in; but I will take one dollar for that book instead."

The man laughed, took out his wallet, and handed Bobby the dollar, probably quite as much because he had a high appreciation of his smartness, as from any desire to possess the book.

"Won't you take one?" asked Bobby, appealing to another of the men, who was apparently not more than twenty-four years of age.

"No; I can't read," replied he, roguishly.

"Let your wife read it to you then."

"My wife?"

"Certainly; she knows how to read, I will warrant."

"How do you know I have got a wife?"

"O, well, a fellow as good looking and good natured as you are could not have resisted till this time."

"Has you, Tom," added the oldest shoemaker.

"I cave in;" and he handed over the dollar, and laid the book upon his bench.

Bobby looked at the third man with some interest. He had said nothing, and scarcely heeded the fun

which was passing between the little merchant and
his companions. He was apparently absorbed in his
examination of the book. He was a different kind
of person from the others, and Bobby's instinctive
knowledge of human nature assured him that he was
not to be gained by flattery or by smart sayings; so
he placed himself in front of him, and patiently waited
in silence for him to complete his examination.

"You will find that he is a hard one," put in one
of the others.

Bobby made no reply, and the two men who had
bought books resumed their work. For five minutes
our hero stood waiting for the man to finish his investigation into the merits of "The Wayfarer."
Something told him not to say any thing to this
person; and he had some doubts about his pur
chasing.

"I will take one," said the last shoemaker, as he
handed Bobby the dollar.

"I am much obliged to you, gentlemen,' said Bobby, as he closed his valise. "When I come this way
again I shall certainly call."

"Do; you have done what no other pedler ever
did in this shop."

'I shall take no credit to myself. The fact is, you are men of intelligence, and you want good books."

Bobby picked up his valise and left the shop, satisfied with those who occupied it, and satisfied with himself.

"Eight shillings!" exclaimed he, when he got into the road. "Pretty good hour's work, I should say."

Bobby trudged along till he came to a very large, elegant house, evidently dwelt in by one of the nabobs of B——. Inspired by past successes, he walked boldly up to the front door, and rang the bell.

"Is Mr. Whiting in?" asked Bobby, who had read the name on the door plate.

"Colonel Whiting *is* in," replied the servant, who had opened the door.

"I should like to see him for a moment, if he isn't busy."

"Walk in;" and for some reason or other the servant chuckled a great deal as she admitted him.

She conducted him to a large, elegantly furnished parlor, where Bobby proceeded to take out his books for the inspection of the nabob, whom the servant promised to send to the parlor.

In a moment Colonel Whiting entered. He was a large, fat man, about fifty years old. He looked at the little book merchant with a frown that would have annihilated a boy less spunky than our hero. Bobby was not a little inflated by the successes of the morning, and if Julius Cæsar or Napoleon Bonaparte had stood before him then, he would not have flinched a hair — much less in the presence of no greater magnate than the nabob of B——.

"Good morning, Colonel Whiting. I hope you are well this beautiful morning," Bobby began.

I must confess I think this was a little too familiar for a boy of thirteen to a gentleman of fifty, whom he had never seen before in his life; but it must be remembered that Bobby had done a great deal the week before, that on the preceding night he had slept in Chestnut Street, and that he had just sold four copies of "The Wayfarer." He was inclined to be smart, and some folks hate smart boys.

The nabob frowned; his cheek reddened with anger; but he did not condescend to make any reply to the smart speech.

"I have taken the liberty to call upon you this

morning, to see if you did not wish to purchase a copy of 'The Wayfarer'— a new book just issued from the press, which people say is to be the book of the season."

My young readers need not suppose this was an unpromptu speech, for Bobby had studied upon it all the time he was coming from Boston in the cars. It would be quite natural for a boy who had enjoyed no greater educational advantages than our hero to consider how he should address people into whose presence his calling would bring him; and he had prepared several little addresses of this sort, for the several different kinds of people whom he expected to encounter. The one he had just "got off" was designed for the "upper crust."

When he had delivered the speech, he approached the indignant, frowning nabob, and with a low bow, offered him a copy of "The Wayfarer."

"Boy," said Colonel Whiting, raising his arm with majestic dignity, and pointing to the door, — "boy do you see that door?"

Bobby looked at the door, and, somewhat astonished replied that he did see it, that it was a very handsome door, and he would inquire whether it was black walnut, or only painted in imitation thereof.

"Do you see that door?" thundered the nabob, swelling with rage at the cool impudence of the boy

"Certainly I do, sir; my eyesight is excellent."

"Then use it!"

"Thank you, sir; I have no use for it. Probaoly it will be of more service to you than to me."

"Will you clear out, or shall I kick you out?" gasped the enraged magnate of B———.

"I will save you that trouble, sir; I will go, sir. I see we have both made a mistake."

"Mistake? What do you mean by that, you young puppy? You are a little impudent, thieving scoundrel!"

"That's your mistake, sir. I took you for a gentleman, sir; and that was my mistake."

"Ha, ha, ha!" laughed a sweet, musical voice, and at that moment a beautiful young lady rushed up to the angry colonel, and threw her arms around his neck.

"The jade!" muttered he.

"I have caught you in a passion again, uncle;"

and the lady kissed the old gentleman's anger-reddened cheek, which seemed to restore him at once to himself.

"It was enough to make a minister swear," said he, in apology.

"No, it wasn't, uncle; the boy was a little pert, it is true; but you ought to have laughed at him, instead of getting angry. I heard the whole of it."

"Pert?" said Bobby to himself. "What the deuse does she mean by that?"

"Very well, you little minx; I will pay the penalty."

"Come here, Master Pert," said the lady to Bobby.

Bobby bowed, approached the lady, and began to feel very much embarrassed.

"My uncle," she continued, "is one of the best hearted men in the world — ain't you, uncle?"

"Go on, you jade!"

"I love him, as I would my own father; but he will sometimes get into a passion. Now, you provoked him."

"Indeed, ma'am, I hadn't the least idea of saying

any thing uncivil," pleaded Bobby. " I studied to be as polite as possible."

" I dare say. You were too important, too pompous, for a boy to an old gentleman like uncle, who is really one of the best men in the world. Now, if you hadn't *studied* to be polite, you would have done very well."

" Indeed, ma'am, I am a poor boy, trying to make a little money to help my mother. I am sure I meant no harm."

" I know you didn't. So you are selling books to help your mother?"

" Yes, ma'am."

She inquired still further into the little merchant's history, and seemed to be very much interested in him.

In a frolic, a few days before, Bobby learned from her, Colonel Whiting had agreed to pay any penalty she might name, the next time he got into a passion.

" Now, young man, what book have you to sell?" asked the lady.

" ' The Wayfarer.' "

" How many have you in your valise?"

"Eight."

"Very well; now, uncle, I decree, as the penalty of your indiscretion, that you purchase the whole stock."

"I submit."

"'The Wayfarer' promises to be an excellent book; and I can name at least half a dozen persons who will thank you for a copy, uncle."

Colonel Whiting paid Bobby eight dollars, who left the contents of his valise on the centre table, and then departed, astounded at his good fortune, and fully resolved never to be too smart again.

CHAPTER XI.

IN WHICH BOBBY STRIKES A BALANCE, AND RE-
TURNS TO RIVERDALE.

OUR hero had learned a lesson which experience alone could teach him. The consciousness of that "something within him" inclined him to be a little too familiar with his elders; but then it gave him confidence in himself, and imparted courage to go forward in the accomplishment of his mission. His interview with Colonel Whiting and the gentle but plain rebuke of his niece had set him right, and he realized that, while he was doing a man's work, he was still a boy. He had now a clearer perception of what is due to the position and dignity of those upon whom fortune has smiled.

Bobby wanted to be a man, and it is not strange that he should sometimes fancy he was a man. He had an idea, too, that all men are born free and equal;" and he could not exactly see why a nabob was entitled to any more respect and consideration than a poor man. It was a lesson he was compelled to learn, though some folks live out their lifetimes without ever finding out that.

" 'Tis wealth, good sir, makes honorable men." Some people think a rich man is no better than a poor man, except so far as he behaves himself better. It is strange how stupid some people are!

Bobby had no notion of cringing to any man, and he felt as independent as the Declaration of Independence itself. But then the beautiful lady had told him that he was pert and forward; and when he thought it over, he was willing to believe she was right. Colonel Whiting was an old man, compared with himself; and he had some faith, at least in theory, in the Spartan virtue of respect for the aged. Probably the nabob of B—— would have objected to being treated with respect on account of his age; and Bobby would have been equally unwilling to acknowledge that he treated him with peculiar respect on account of his wealth or position.

Perhaps the little merchant had an instinctive per

ception of expediency — that he should sell more books by being less familiar: at any rate he determined never again to use the flowery speeches he had arranged for the upper crust.

He had sold a dozen books; and possibly this fact made him more willing to compromise the matter than he would otherwise have been. This was, after all, the great matter for congratulation, and with a light heart he hurried back to the railroad station to procure another supply.

We cannot follow him into every house where his calling led him. He was not always as fortunate as in the instances we have mentioned. Sometimes all his arguments were unavailing, and after he had spent half an hour of valuable time in setting forth the merits of "The Wayfarer," he was compelled to retire without having effected a sale. Sometimes, too, he was rudely repulsed; hard epithets were applied to him; old men and old women, worried out by the continued calls of pedlers, sneered at him, or shut the door in his face; but Bobby was not disheartened. He persevered, and did not allow these little trials to discompose or discourage him.

By one o'clock on the first day of his service he had sold eighteen books, which far exceeded even his most sanguine expectations. By this time he began to feel the want of his dinner; but there was no tavern or eating house at hand, and he could not think of leaving the harvest to return to the railroad station; so he bought a sheet of gingerbread and a piece of cheese at a store, and seating himself near a brook by the side of the road, he bolted his simple meal, as boys are very apt to do when they are excited.

When he had finished, he took out his account book, and entered, "Dinner, 10 cents." Resuming his business, he disposed of the remaining six books in his valise by the middle of the afternoon, and was obliged to return for another supply.

About six o'clook he entered the house of a mechanic, just as the family were sitting down to tea. He recommended his book with so much energy, that the wife of the mechanic took a fancy to him, and not only purchased one, but invited him to tea. Bobby accepted the invitation, and in the course of the meal, the good lady drew from him the details of his history, which he very modestly related, for though he sometimes fancied himself a man, he was not the boy to boast of his exploits. His host was so much pleased with him, that he begged him to spend the night with them. Bobby had been thinking how and where he should spend the night, and the matter had given him no little concern. He did not wish to go to the hotel, for it looked like a very smart house, and he reasoned that he should have to pay pretty roundly for accommodations there. These high prices would eat up his profits, and he seriously deliberated whether it would not be better for him to sleep under a tree than pay fifty cents for a lodging.

If I had been there I should have told him that a man loses nothing in the long run by taking good care of himself. He must eat well and sleep well, in order to do well and be well. But I suppose Bobby would have told me that it was of no use to pay a quarter extra for sleeping on a gilded bedstead, since the room would be so dark he could not see the gilt even if he wished to do so. I could not have said any thing to such a powerful argument, so I am very glad the mechanic's wife set the matter at rest by offering him a bed in her house.

He spent a very pleasant evening with the family, who made him feel entirely at home, they were so kind and so plain spoken. Before he went to bed, he entered under the book account, " By twenty-six Wayfarers, sold this day, $26.00."

He had done a big day's work, much bigger than he could hope to do again. He had sold more than one half of his whole stock, and at this rate he should be out of books the next day. At first he thought he would send for another lot; but he could not judge yet what his average daily sales would be, and finally concluded not to do so. What he had might last till Friday or Saturday. He intended to go home on the latter day, and he could bring them with him on his return without expense. This was considerable of an argument for a boy to manage; but Bobby was satisfied with it, and went to sleep, wondering what his mother, Squire Lee, and Annie were thinking of about that time.

After breakfast the next morning he resumed his ravels. He was as enthusiastic as ever, and pressed

* The Wayfarer" with so much earnestness that he sold a book in nearly every house he visited. People seemed to be more interested in the little merchant than in his stock, and taking advantage of this kind feeling towards him, he appealed to them with so much eloquence that few could resist it.

The result of the day's sales was fifteen copies, which Bobby entered in the book account with the most intense satisfaction. He had outdone the boy who had passed through Riverdale, but he had little hope that the harvest would always be so abundant.

He often thought of this boy, from whom he had obtained the idea he was now carrying out. That boy had stopped over night at the little black house, and slept with him. He had asked for lodging, and offered to pay for it, as well as for his supper and breakfast. Why couldn't he do the same? He liked the suggestion, and from that time, wherever he happened to be, he asked for lodging, or the meal he required, and he always proposed to pay for what he had, but very few would take any thing.

On Friday noon he had sold out. Returning to the railroad station, he found that the train would not leave for the city for an hour; so he improved the time in examining and balancing his accounts. The book sales amounted to just fifty dollars, and after his ticket to Boston was paid for, his expenses would amount to one dollar and fifty cents, leaving a balance in his favor of fifteen dollars. He was overjoyed with the result, and pictured the astonishment with which his mother, Squire Lee, and Annie would listen to the history of his excursion.

After four o'clock that afternoon he entered the store of Mr. Bayard, bag and baggage. On his arrival in the city, he was considerably exercised in mind to know how he should get the trunk to his destination. He was too economical to pay a cartman a quarter; but what would have seemed mean in a man was praiseworthy in a boy laboring for a noble end.

Probably a great many of my young readers in Bobby's position, thinking that sixteen dollars, which our hero had in his pocket, was a mint of money, would have been in favor of being a little magnificent — of taking a carriage and going up-town in state. Bobby had not the least desire to "swell;" so he settled the matter by bargaining with a little ragged fellow to help him carry the trunk to Mr. Bayard's store for fourpence.

"How do you do, Mr. Timmins?" said Bobby to the spruce clerk, as he deposited the trunk upon the floor, and handed the ragged boy the fourpence.

"Ah, Bobby!" exclaimed Mr. Timmins. "Have you sold out?"

"All clean. Is Mr. Bayard in?"

"In the office. But how do you like it?"

"First rate."

"Well, every one to his taste; but I don't see how any one who has any regard for his dignity can stick himself into every body's house. I couldn't do it, I know."

"I don't stand for the dignity."

"Ah, well, there is a difference in folks."

"That's a fact," replied Bobby, as he hurried to the office of Mr. Bayard, leaving Mr. Timmins to sun himself in his own dignity.

The bookseller was surprised to see him so soon, but he gave him a cordial reception.

"I didn't expect you yet," said he. "Way du you come back? Have you got sick of the business?"

"Sick of it! No, sir."

"What have you come back for then?"

"Sold out, sir."

"Sold out! You have done well!"

"Better than I expected."

"I had no idea of seeing you till to-morrow night; and I thought you would have books enough to begin the next week with. You have done bravely."

"If I had had twenty more, I could have sold them before to-morrow night. Now, sir, if you please, I will pay you for those books — thirty-three dollars and fifty cents."

"You had better keep that, Bobby. I will trust you as long as you wish."

"If you please, sir, I had rather pay it;" and the little merchant, as proud as a lord, handed over the amount.

"I like your way of doing business, Bobby. Nothng helps a man's credit so much as paying promptly. Now tell me some of your adventures — or we will reserve them till this evening, for I am sure Ellen will be delighted to hear them."

" I think I shall go to Riverdale this afternoon. The cars leave at half past five."

" Very well; you have an hour to spare."

Bobby related to his kind friend the incidents of his excursion, including his interview with Colonel Whiting and his niece, which amused the bookseller very much. He volunteered some good advice, which Bobby received in the right spirit, and with a determination to profit by it.

At half past five he took the cars for home, and before dark was folded in his mother's arms. The little black house seemed doubly dear to him now that he had been away from it a few days. His mother and all the children were so glad to see him that it seemed almost worth his while to go away for the pleasure of meeting them on his return

CHAPTER XII.

IN WHICH BOBBY ASTONISHES SUNDRY PERSONS AND PAYS PART OF HIS NOTE.

"Now tell me, Bobby, how you have made out,' said Mrs. Bright, as the little merchant seated himself at the supper table. "You cannot have done much, for you have only been gone five days."

"I have done pretty well, mother," replied Bobby, mysteriously; "pretty well, considering that I am only a boy."

"I didn't expect to see you till to-morrow night."

"I sold out, and had to come home."

"That may be, and still you may not have done much."

"I don't pretend that I have done much."

"How provoking you are! Why don't you tell me, Bobby, what you have done?"

"Wait a minute, mother, til. I have done my

supper, and then I will show you the footings in my ledger."

" Your ledger!"

' Yes, my ledger. I keep a ledger now."

" You are a great man, Mr. Robert Bright," laughed his mother. " I suppose the people took their hats off when they saw you coming."

" Not exactly, mother."

" Perhaps the governor came out to meet you when he heard you was on the road."

" Perhaps he did; I didn't see him, however This apple pie tastes natural, mother. It is a great luxury to get home after one has been travelling."

" Very likely."

" No place like home, after all is done and said. Who was the fellow that wrote that song, mother?"

" I forget; the paper said he spent a great many years in foreign parts. My sake! Bobby; one would think by your talk that you had been away from home for a year."

" It seems like a year," said he, as he transferred another quarter of the famous apple pie to his plate

"I miss home very much. I don't more than half like being among strangers so much."

"It is your own choice; no one wants you to go away from home."

"I must pay my debts, any how. Don't I owe Squire Lee sixty dollars?"

"But I can pay that."

"It is my affair, you see."

"If it is your affair, then I owe you sixty dollars."

"No, you don't; I calculate to pay my board now. I am old enough and big enough to do something."

"You have done something ever since you was old enough to work."

"Not much; I don't wonder that miserable old hunker of a Hardhand twitted me about it. By the way, have you heard any thing from him?"

"Not a thing."

"He has got enough of us, I reckon."

"You mustn't insult him, Bobby, if you happen to see him."

"Never fear me."

"You know the Bible says we must love our

enemies, and pray for them that despitefully use us and persecute us."

"I should pray that the Old Nick might get him."

"No, Bobby; I hope you haven't forgot all your Sunday school lessons."

"I was wrong, mother," replied Bobby, a little moved. "I did not mean so. I shall try to think as well of him as I can; but I can't help thinking, if all the world was like him, what a desperate hard time we should have of it."

"We must thank the Lord that he has given us so many good and true men."

"Such as Squire Lee, for instance," added Bobby, as he rose from the table and put his chair back against the wall. "The squire is fit to be a king; and though I believe in the Constitution and the Declaration of Independence, I wouldr t mind seeing a crown upon his head."

"He will receive his crown in due time," replied Mrs. Bright, piously.

"The squire?"

"The crown of rejoicing, I mean.'

"Just so; the squire is a nice man; and I know another just like him."

"Who!"

"Mr. Bayard; they are as near alike as two peas."

"I am dying to know about your journey."

"Wait a minute, mother, till we clear away the supper things;" and Bobby took hold, as he had been accustomed, to help remove and wash the dishes.

"You needn't help now, Bobby."

"Yes, I will, mother."

Some how our hero's visit to the city did not seem to produce the usual effect upon him; for a great many boys, after they had been abroad, would have scorned to wash dishes and wipe them. A week in town has made many a boy so smart that you couldn't touch him with a ten foot pole. It starches them up so stiff that sometimes they don't know their own mothers, and deem it a piece of condescension to speak a word to the patriarch in a blue frock who had the honor of supporting them in childhood.

Bobby was none of this sort. We lament that he

had a habit of talking big — that is, of talking about business affairs in a style a little beyond his years. But he was modest to a fault, paradoxical as it may seem. He was always blushing when any body spoke a pretty thing about him. Probably the circumstances of his position elevated him above the sphere of the mere boy; he had spent but little time in play, and his attention had been directed at all times to the wants of his mother. He had thought a great deal about business, especially since the visit of the boy who sold books to the little black house.

Some boys are born merchants, and from their earliest youth have a genius for trade. They think of little else. They "play shop" before they wear jackets, and drive a barter trade in jackknives, whistles, tops, and fishing lines long before they get into their teens. They are shrewd even then, and obtain a taste for commerce before they are old enough to know the meaning of the word.

We saw a boy in school, not long since, give the value of eighteen cents for a little stunted quince — boys have a taste for raw quinces, strange as it may seem. Undoubtedly he had no talent for trade, and would make a very indifferent tin pedler. Our hero was shrewd. He always got the best end of the bargain; though, I am happy to say, his integrity was too unyielding to let him cheat his fellows.

We have made this digression so that my young readers may know why Bobby was so much given to big talk. The desire to do something worthy of a good son turned his attention to matters above his sphere; and thinking of great things, he had come to talk great things. It was not a bad fault, after all. Boys need not necessarily be frivolous. Play is a good thing, an excellent thing, in its place, and is as much a part of the boy's education as his grammar and arithmetic. It not only develops his muscles, but enlarges his mental capacity; it not only fills with excitement the idle hours of the long day, but it sharpens the judgment, and helps to fit the boy for the active duties of life.

It need not be supposed, because Bobby had to turn his attention to serious things, that he was not fond of fun; that he could not or did not play. At a game of round ball, he was a lucky fellow who secured him upon his side; for the same energy which made him a useful son rendered him a desirable hand in a difficult game.

When the supper things were all removed, the dishes washed and put away, Bobby drew out his pocket memorandum book. It was a beautiful article, and Mrs. Bright was duly astonished at its gilded leaves and the elegant workmanship. Very likely her first impulse was to reprove her son for such a piece of reckless extravagance; but this matter was set right by Bobby's informing her how it came into his possession.

"Here is my ledger, mother," he said, handing her the book.

Mrs. Bright put on her spectacles, and after bestowing a careful scrutiny upon the memorandum book, turned to the accounts.

"Fifty books!" she exclaimed, as she read the first entry.

"Yes, mother; and I sold them all."

"Fifty dollars!"

"But I had to pay for the books out of that."

"To be sure you had; but I suppose you made as much as ten cents a piece on them, and that would be— let me see; ten times fifty ——."

"But I made more than that, I hope."

" How much ? "

The proud young merchant referred her to the profit and loss account, which exhibited a balance of fifteen dollars.

" Gracious ! Three dollars a day ! "

" Just so, mother. Now I will pay you the dollar I borrowed of you when I went away."

" You didn't borrow it of me."

" But I shall pay it."

Mrs. Bright was astonished at this unexpected and gratifying result. If she had discovered a gold mine in the cellar of the little black house, it could not have afforded her so much satisfaction; for this money was the reward of her son's talent and energy. Her own earnings scarcely ever amounted to more than three or four dollars a week, and Bobby, a boy of thirteen, had come home with fifteen for five days' work. She could scarcely believe the evidence of her own senses, and she ceased to wonder that he talked big.

It was nearly ten o'clock when the widow and her son went to bed, so deeply were they interested in discussing our hero's affairs. He had intended to call upon Squire Lee that night, but the time passed away so rapidly that he was obliged to defer it till the next day.

After breakfast the following morning, he hastened to pay the intended visit. There was a tumult of strange emotions in his bosom as he knocked at the squire's door. He was proud of the success he had achieved, and even then his cheek burned under the anticipated commendations which his generous friend would bestow upon him. Besides, Annie would be glad to see him, for she had expressed such a desire when they parted on the Monday preceding. I don't think that Bobby cherished any silly ideas, but the sympathy of the little maiden fell not coldly or unwelcomely upon his warm heart. In coming from the house he had placed his copy of "The Wayfarer" under his arm, for Annie was fond of reading; and on the way over, he had pictured to himself the pleasure she would derive from reading *his* book.

Of course he received a warm welcome from the squire and his daughter. Each of them had bestowed more than a thought upon the little wanderer as he went from house to house, and more than once they had conversed together about him.

"Well, Bobby, how is trade in the book line?" asked the squire, after the young pilgrim had been cordially greeted.

"Pretty fair," replied Bobby, with as much indifference as he could command, though it was hard even to seem indifferent then and there.

"Where have you been travelling?"

"In B——."

"Fine place. Books sell well there?"

"Very well; in fact, I sold out all my stock by noon yesterday."

"How many books did you carry?"

"Fifty."

"You did well."

"I should think you did!" added Annie, with an enthusiasm which quite upset all Bobby's assumed indifference. "Fifty books!"

"Yes. Miss Annie; and I have brought you a copy of the book I have been selling; I thought you would like to read it. It is a splendid work, and will be *the* book of the season."

"I shall be delighted to read it," replied Annie, taking the proffered volume. "It looks real good," she continued, as she turned over the leaves.

"It is first rate; I have read it through."

"It was very kind of you to think of me when you have so much business on your mind," added she, with a roguish smile.

"I shall never have so much business on my mind that I cannot think of my friends," replied Bobby, so gallantly and so smartly that it astonished himself.

"I was just thinking what I should read next; I am *so* glad you have come."

"Never mind her, Bobby; all she wanted was the book," interposed Squire Lee, laughing.

"Now, pa!"

"Then I shall bring her one very often."

"You are too bad, pa," said Annie, who, like most young ladies just entering their teens, resented any imputation upon the immaculateness of human love, or human friendship.

"I have got a little money for you, Squire Lee," continued Bobby, thinking it time the subject was changed.

He took out his gilded memorandum book, whose elegant appearance rather startled the squire, and from its "treasury department" extracted the little roll of bills, representing an aggregate of ten dollars which he had carefully reserved for his creditor.

"Never mind that, Bobby," replied the squire. "You will want all your capital to do business with."

"I must pay my debts before I think of any thing else."

"A very good plan, Bobby, but this is an exception to the general rule."

"No, sir, I think not. If you please, I insist upon paying you ten dollars on my note."

"O, well, if you insist, I suppose I can't help myself."

"I would rather pay it, I shall feel so much better.'

"You want to indorse it on the note, I suppose."

That was just what Bobby wanted. Indorsed on the note was the idea, and our hero had often passed that expression through his mind. There was something gratifying in the act to a man of business integrity like himself; it was discharging a sacred obligation, — he had already come to deem it a sacred duty to pay one's debts, — and as the squire wrote the indorsement across the back of the note, he felt more like a hero than ever before.

"'Pay as you go' is an excellent idea; John Randolph called it the philosopher's stone," added Squire Lee, as he returned the note to his pocket book.

"That is what I mean to do just as soon as I can."

"You will do, Bobby."

The young merchant spent nearly the whole forenoon at the squire's, and declined an invitation to dinner only on the plea that his mother would wait for him.

CHAPTER XIII.

IN WHICH BOBBY DECLINES A COPARTNERSHIP AND VISITS B—— AGAIN.

AFTER dinner Bobby performed his Saturday afternoon chores as usual. He split wood enough to last for a week, so that his mother might not miss him too much, and then, feeling a desire to visit his favorite resorts in the vicinity, he concluded to go a fishing. The day was favorable, the sky being overcast and the wind very light. After digging a little box of worms in the garden back of the house, he shouldered his fish pole; and certainly no one would have suspected that he was a distinguished travelling merchant. He was fond of fishing, and it is a remarkable coincidence that Daniel Webster, and many other famous men, have manifested a decided passion for this exciting sport. No doubt a fondness for angling is a peculiarity of genius; and if being an expert fisherman makes a great man, then our hero was a great man.

He had scarcely seated himself on his favorite rock, and dropped his line into the water, before he saw Tom Spicer approaching the spot. The bully had never been a welcome companion. There was no sympathy between them. They could never agree, for their views, opinions, and tastes were always conflicting.

Bobby had not seen Tom since he left him to crawl out of the ditch on the preceding week, and he had good reason to believe that he should not be regarded with much favor. Tom was malicious and revengeful, and our hero was satisfied that the blow which had prostrated him in the ditch would not be forgotten till it had been atoned for. He was prepared, therefore, for any disagreeable scene which might occur.

There was another circumstance also which rendered the bully's presence decidedly unpleasant at this time — an event that had occurred during his absence, the particulars of which he had received from his mother.

Tom's father, who was a poor man, and addicted to

intemperance, had lost ten dollars. He had brought it home, and, as he affirmed, placed it in one of the bureau drawers. The next day it could not be found. Spicer, for some reason, was satisfied that Tom had taken it; but the boy stoutly and persistently denied it. No money was found upon him, however, and it did not appear that he had spent any at the stores in Riverdale Centre.

The affair created some excitement in the vicinity, for Spicer made no secret of his suspicions, and publicly accused Tom of the theft. He did not get much sympathy from any except his pot companions; for there was no evidence but his bare and unsupported statement to substantiate the grave accusation. Tom had been in the room when the money was placed in the drawer, and, as his father asserted, had watched him closely while he deposited the bills under the clothing. No one else could have taken it. These were the proofs. But people generally believed that Spicer had carried no money home, especially as it was known that he was intoxicated on the night in question; and that the alleged theft was only a ruse to satisfy certain importunate creditors.

Every body knew that Tom was bad enough to steal, even from his father; from which my readers can understand that it is an excellent thing to have a good reputation. Bobby knew that he would lie and use profane language; that he spent his Sundays by the river, or in roaming through the woods; and that he played truant from school as often as the fear of the rod would permit; and the boy that would do all these things certainly would steal if he got a good chance. Our hero's judgment, therefore, of the case was not favorable to the bully, and he would have thanked him to stay away from the river while he was there.

"Hallo, Bob! How are you?" shouted Tom, when he had come within hailing distance.

"Very well," replied Bobby, rather coolly.

"Been to Boston, they say."

"Yes."

"Well, how did you like it?" continued Tom as he seated himself on the rock near our hero.

"First rate."

"Been to work there?"

"No."

" What have you been doing?"

" Travelling about."

" What doing?"

" Selling books."

" Was you, though? Did you sell any?"

" Yes, a few."

" How many?"

" O, about fifty."

" You didn't, though — did you? How much did you make?"

" About fifteen dollars."

" By jolly! You are a smart one, Bobby. There are not many fellows that would have done that."

" Easy enough," replied Bobby, who was not a little surprised at this warm commendation from one whom he regarded as his enemy.

" You had to buy the books first — didn't you?" asked Tom, who began to manifest a deep interest in the trade.

' Of course; no one will give you the books."

" What do you pay for them?"

" I buy them so as to make a profit on them," answered Bobby, who, like a discreet merchant, was not disposed to be too communicative.

" That business would suit me first rate."

" It is pretty hard work."

" I don't care for that. Don't you believe I could do something in this line?"

" I don't know; perhaps you could."

" Why not, as well as you?"

This was a hard question; and, as Bobby did not wish to be uncivil, he talked about a big pout he hauled in at that moment, instead of answering it. He was politic, and deprecated the anger of the bully; so, though Tom plied him pretty hard, he did not receive much satisfaction.

" You see, Tom," said he, when he found that his companion insisted upon knowing the cost of the books, " this is a publisher's secret; and I dare say they would not wish every one to know the cost of books. We sell them for a dollar apiece."

" Humph! You needn't be so close about it. I'll bet I can find out."

" I have no doubt you can; only, you see, I don't want to tell what I am not sure they would be willing I should tell."

Tom took a slate pencil from his pocket, and

commenced ciphering on the smooth rock upon which he sat.

'You say you sold fifty books?"

"Yes."

"Well; if you made fifteen dollars out of fifty, that is thirty cents apiece."

Bobby was a little mortified when he perceived that he had unwittingly exposed the momentous secret. He had not given Tom credit for so much sagacity as he had displayed in his inquiries; and as he had fairly reached his conclusion, he was willing he should have the benefit of it.

"You sold them at a dollar apiece. Thirty from a hundred leaves seventy. They cost you seventy cents each — didn't they?"

"Sixty-seven," replied Bobby, yielding the point.

"Enough said, Bob; I am going into that business, any how."

"I am willing."

"Of course you are; suppose we go together," suggested Tom, who had not used all this conciliation without having a purpose in view.

"We could do nothing together."

"I should like to get out with you just once, only to see how it is done."

"You can find out for yourself, as I did."

"Don't be mean Bob."

"Mean? I am not mean."

"I don't say you are. We have always been good friends, you know."

Bobby did not know it; so he looked at the other with a smile which expressed all he meant to say.

"You hit me a smart dig the other day, I know; but I don't mind that. I was in the wrong then, and I am willing to own it," continued Tom, with an appearance of humility.

This was an immense concession for Tom to make, and Bobby was duly affected by it. Probably it was the first time the bully had ever owned he was in the wrong.

"The fact is, Bob, I always liked you; and you know I licked Ben Dowse for you."

"That was two for yourself and one for me; besides, I didn't want Ben thrashed."

"But he deserved it. Didn't he tell the master you were whispering in school?"

"I was whispering; so he told the truth."

"It was mean to blow on a fellow, though."

"The master asked him if I whispered to him; of course he ought not to lie about it. But he told of you at the same time."

"I know it; but I wouldn't have licked him on my own account."

"*Perhaps* you wouldn't."

"I know I wouldn't. But, I say, Bobby, where do you buy your books?"

"At Mr. Bayard's, in Washington Street."

"He will sell them to me at the same price — won't he?"

"I don't know."

"When are you going again?"

"Monday."

"Won't you let me go with you, Bob?"

"Let you? Of course you can go where you please; it is none of my business."

Bobby did not like the idea of having such a copartner as Tom Spicer, and he did not like to tell him so. If he did, he would have to give his reason for declining the proposition, and that would make Tom mad, and perhaps provoke him to quarrel.

The fish bit well, and in an hour's time Bobby had a mess. As he took his basket and walked home, the young ruffian followed him. He could not get rid of him till he reached the gate in front of the little black house; and even there Tom begged him to stop a few moments. Our hero was in a hurry, and in the easiest manner possible got rid of this aspirant for mercantile honors.

We have no doubt a journal of Bobby's daily life would be very interesting to our young readers; but the fact that some of his most stirring adventures are yet to be related admonishes us to hasten forward more rapidly.

On Monday morning Bobby bade adieu to his mother again, and started for Boston. He fully expected to encounter Tom on the way, who, he was afraid, would persist in accompanying him on his tour. As before, he stopped at Squire Lee's to bid him and Annie good by.

The little maiden had read " The Wayfarer " more than half through, and was very enthusiastic in her expression of the pleasure she derived from it. She promised to send it over to his house when she had finished it, and hoped he would bring his stock to Riverdale, so that she might again replenish her library. Bobby thought of something just then, and the thought brought forth a harvest on the following Saturday, when he returned.

When he had shaken hands with the squire and was about to depart, he received a piece of news which gave him food for an hour's serious reflection.

" Did you hear about Tom Spicer?" asked Squire Lee.

" No, sir; what about him?"

" Broken his arm."

" Broken his arm! Gracious! How did it happen?" exclaimed Bobby, the more astonished because he had been thinking of Tom since he had left home.

" He was out in the woods yesterday, where boys should not be on Sundays, and, in climbing a tree after a bird's nest, he fell to the ground."

" I am sorry for him," replied Bobby, musing.

" So am I; but if he had been at home, or at church, where he should have been, it would not have happened. If I had any boys, I would lock them up in their chambers if I could not keep them at home Sundays."

"Poor Tom!" mused Bobby, recalling the conversation he had had with him on Saturday, and then wishing that he had been a little more pliant with him.

"It is too bad; but I must say I am more sorry for his poor mother than I am for him," added the squire. "However, I hope it will do him good, and be a lesson he will remember as long as he lives."

Bobby bade the squire and Annie adieu again, and resumed his journey towards the railroad station. His thoughts were busy with Tom Spicer's case. The reason why he had not joined him, as he expected and feared he would, was now apparent He pitied him, for he realized that he must endure a great deal of pain before he could again go out; but he finally dismissed the matter with the squire's sage reflection, that he hoped the calamity would be a good lesson to him.

The young merchant did not walk to Boston this time, for he had come to the conclusion that, in the six hours it would take him to travel to the city on foot, the profit on the books he could sell would be more than enough to pay his fare, to say nothing of the fatigue and the expense of shoe leather.

Before noon he was at B—— again, as busy as ever in driving his business. The experience of the former week was of great value to him. He visited people belonging to all spheres in society, and, though he was occasionally repulsed or treated with incivility, he was not conscious in a single instance of offending any person's sense of propriety.

He was not as fortunate as during the previous week, and it was Saturday noon before he had sold out the sixty books he carried with him. The net profit for this week was fourteen dollars, with which he was abundantly pleased.

Mr. Bayard again commended him in the warmest terms for his zeal and promptness. Mr. Timmins was even more civil than the last time, and when Bobby asked the price of Moore's Poems, he actually offered to sell it to him for thirty-three per cent. less than the retail price. The little merchant was on the point of purchasing it, when Mr. Bayard inquired what he wanted.

"I am going to buy this book," replied Bobby

"Moore's Poems?"

"Yes, sir."

Mr. Bayard took from a glass case an elegantly bound copy of the same work — morocco, full gilt — and handed it to our hero.

"I shall make you a present of this. Are you an admirer of Moore?"

"No, sir; not exactly — that is, I don't know much about it; but Annie Lee does, and I want to get the book for her."

Bobby's cheeks reddened as he turned the leaves of the beautiful volume, putting his head down to the page to hide his confusion.

"Annie Lee?" said Mr. Bayard with a quizzing smile. "I see how it is. Rather young, Bobby."

"Her father has been very good to me and to my mother; and so has Annie, for that matter. Squire Lee would be a great deal more pleased if I should make Annie a present than if I made him one. I feel grateful to him, and I want to let it out some how."

"That's right, Bobby; always remember your friends. Timmins, wrap up this book."

Bobby protested with all his might; but the book

seller insisted that he should give Annie this beautifu. edition, and he was obliged to yield the point.

That evening he was at the little black house again, and his mother examined his ledger with a great deal of pride and satisfaction. That evening, too, another ten dollars was indorsed on the note, and Annie received that elegant copy of Moore's Poems.

CHAPTER XIV.

IN WHICH BOBBY'S AIR CASTLE IS UPSET AND
TOM SPICER TAKES TO THE WOODS.

DURING the next four weeks Bobby visited various places in the vicinity of Boston; and at the end of that time he had paid the whole of the debt he owed Squire Lee. He had the note in his memorandum book, and the fact that he had achieved his first great purpose afforded him much satisfaction. Now he owed no man any thing, and he felt as though he could hold up his head among the best people in the world.

The little black house was paid for, and Bobby was proud that his own exertions had released his mother from her obligation to her hard creditor. Mr. Hardhand could no longer insult and abuse her.

The apparent results which Bobby had accomplished, however, were as nothing compared with the real results. He had developed those energies of character which were to make h m, not only a great business man, but a useful member of society. Besides, there was a moral grandeur in his humble achievements which was more worthy of consideration than the mere worldly success he had obtained. Motives determine the character of deeds. That a boy of thirteen should display so much enterprise and energy was a great thing; but that it should be displayed from pure, unselfish devotion to his mother was a vastly greater thing. Many great achievements are morally insignificant, while many of which the world never hears mark the true hero.

Our hero was not satisfied with what he had done, and far from relinquishing his interesting and profitable employment, his ambition suggested new and wider fields of success. As one ideal, brilliant and glorious in its time, was reached, another more brilliant and more glorious presented itself, and demanded to be achieved. The little black house began to appear rusty and inconvenient; a coat of white paint would marvellously improve its appearance; a set of nice Paris-green blinds would make a palace of it; and a neat fence around it would positively transform the place into a paradise. Yet Bobby was audacious enough to think of these things, and even to promise himself that they should be obtained.

In conversation with Mr. Bayard a few days before, that gentleman had suggested a new field of labor; and it had been arranged that Bobby should visit the State of Maine the following week. On the banks of the Kennebec were many wealthy and important towns, where the intelligence of the people created a demand for books. This time the little merchant was to take two hundred books, and be absent until they were all sold.

On Monday morning he started bright and early for the railroad station. As usual, he called upon Squire Lee, and informed Annie that he should probably be absent three or four weeks. She hoped no accident would happen to him, and that his journey would be crowned with success. Without being sentimental, she was a little sad, for Bobby was a great friend of hers. That elegant copy of Moore's Poems had been gratefully received, and she was so fond of the bard's beautiful and touching melodies that she could never read any of them without thinking of the brave little fellow who had given her the volume; which no one will consider very remarkable, even in a little miss of twelve.

After he had bidden her and her father adieu, he resumed his journey. Of course he was thinking with all his might; but no one need suppose he was wondering how wide the Kennebec River was, or how many books he should sell in the towns upon its banks. Nothing of the kind; though it is enough even for the inquisitive to know that he was thinking of something, and that his thoughts were very interesting, not to say romantic.

"Hallo, Bob!" shouted some one from the road side.

Bobby was provoked; for it is sometimes very uncomfortable to have a pleasant train of thought interrupted. The imagination is buoyant, ethereal, and elevates poor mortals up to the stars sometimes. It was so with Bobby. He was building up some kind of an air castle, and had got up in the clouds amidst the fog and moonshine, and that aggravating voice brought him down, *slap*, upon terra firma.

He looked up and saw Tom Spicer seated upon the fence. In his hand he held a bundle, and had evidently been waiting some time for Bobby's coming.

He had recovered from the illness caused by his broken arm, and people said it had been a good lesson for him, as the squire hoped it would be. Bobby had called upon him two or three times during his confinement to the house; and Tom, either truly repentant for his past errors, or lacking the opportunity at that time to manifest his evil propensities, had stoutly protested that he had "turned over a new leaf," and meant to keep out of the woods on Sunday, stop lying and swearing, and become a good boy.

Bobby commended his good resolutions, and told him he would never want friends while he was true to himself. The right side, he declared, was always th best side. He quoted several instances of men, whose lives he had read in his Sunday school books, to show how happy a good man may be in prison, or when all the world seemed to forsake him.

Tom assured him that he meant to reform and be a good boy; and Bobby told him that when any one meant to turn over a new leaf, it was " now or never.'

If he put it off, he would only grow worse, and the longer the good work was delayed, the more difficult it would be to do it. Tom agreed to all this, and was sure he had reformed.

For these reasons Bobby had come to regard Tom with a feeling of deep interest. He considered him as, in some measure, his disciple, and he felt a personal responsibility in encouraging him to persevere in his good work. Nevertheless Bobby was not exactly pleased to have his fine air castle upset, and to be tipped out of the clouds upon the cold, uncompromising earth again; so the first greeting he gave Tom was not as cordial as it might have been.

" Hallo, Tom! " he replied, rather coolly.

" Been waiting for you this half hour."

" Have you? "

" Yes; ain't you rather late? "

" No; I have plenty of time, though none to spare," answered Bobby; and this was a hint that he must not detain him too long.

" Come along then."

" Where are you going, Tom? " asked Bobby, a little surprised at these words.

"To Boston."

"Are you?"

"I am; that's a fact. You know I spoke to you about going into the book business."

"Not lately."

"But I have been thinking about it all the time."

"What do your father and mother say?"

"O, they are all right."

"Have you asked them?"

"Certainly I have; they are willing I should go with *you*."

"Why didn't you speak of it then?"

"I thought I wouldn't say any thing till the time came. You know you fought shy when I spoke about it before."

And Bobby, notwithstanding the interest he felt in his companion, was a little disposed to "fight shy" now. Tom had reformed, or had pretended to do so; but he was still a raw recruit, and our hero was somewhat fearful that he would run at the first fire.

To the good and true man life is a constant battle. Temptation assails him at almost every point; perils and snares beset him at every step of his mortal pil grimage, so that every day he is called upon to gird on his armor and fight the good fight.

Bobby was no poet; but he had a good idea of this every-day strife with the foes of error and sin that crossed his path. It was a practical conception, but it was truly expressed under the similitude of a battle. There was to be resistance, and he could comprehend that, for his bump of combativeness took cognizance of the suggestion. He was to fight; and that was an idea that stood him in better stead than a whole library of ethical subtilties.

Judging Tom by his own standard, he was afraid he would run — that he wouldn't "stand fire." He had not been drilled. Heretofore, when temptation beset him, he had yielded without even a struggle, and fled from the field without firing a gun. To go out into the great world was a trying event for the raw recruit. He lacked, too, that prestige of success which is worth more than numbers on the field of battle.

Tom had chosen for himself, and he could not send him back. He had taken up the line of march, let it ead him where it might.

"March on! in legions death and sin
  Impatient wait thy conquering hand;
  The foe without, the foe within —
  Thy youthful arm must both withstand."

Bobby had great hopes of him. He felt that he could not well get rid of him, and he saw that it was policy for him to make the best of it.

"Well, Tom, where are you going?" asked Bobby, after he had made up his mind not to object to the companionship of the other.

"I don't know. You have been a good friend to me lately, and I had an idea that you would give me a lift in this business."

"I should be very willing to do so; out what can I do for you?"

"Just show me how the business is done; that's all I want."

"Your father and mother were willing you should come — were they not?"

Bobby had some doubts about this point, and with good reason too. He had called at Tom's house, the day before, and they had gone to church together; but neither he nor his parents had said a word about his going to Boston.

"When did they agree to it?"

"Last night," replied Tom, after a moment's hesitation.

"All right then; but I cannot promise you that Mr. Bayard will let you have the books."

"I can fix that, I reckon," replied Tom, confidently.

"I will speak a good word for you, at any rate."

"That's right, Bob."

"I am going down into the State of Maine this time, and shall be gone three or four weeks."

"So much the better; I always wanted to go down that way."

Tom asked a great many questions about the business and the method of travelling, which Bobby's superior intelligence and more extensive experience enabled him to answer to the entire satisfaction of the other.

When they were within half a mile of the railroad station, they heard a carriage driven at a rapid rate approaching them from the direction of Riverdale.

Tom seemed to be uneasy, and cast frequent glances behind him. In a moment the vehicle was within a short distance of them, and he stopped short in the road to scrutinize the persons in it.

"By jolly!" exclaimed Tom; "my father!"

"What of it?" asked Bobby, surprised by the strange behavior of his companion.

Tom did not wait to reply, but springing over the fence, fled like a deer towards some woods a short distance from the road.

Was it possible? Tom had run away from home. His father had not consented to his going to Boston, and Bobby was mortified to find that his hopeful disciple had been lying to him ever since they left Riverdale. But he was glad the cheat had been exposed.

"That was Tom with you — wasn't it?" asked Mr. Spicer, as he stopped the foaming horse.

"Yes, sir; but he told me you had consented that he should go with me," replied Bobby, a little disturbed by the angry glance of Mr. Spicer's fiery eyes.

"He lied! the young villain! He will catch it for this."

"I would not have let him come with me only for that. I asked him twice over if you were willing, and he said you were."

"You ought to have known better than to believe him," interposed the man who was with Mr. Spicer.

Bobby had some reason for believing him. The fact that Tom had reformed ought to have entitled him to some consideration, and our hero gave him the full benefit of the declaration. To have explained this would have taken more time than he could spare; besides, it was "a great moral question," whose importance Mr. Spicer and his companion would not be likely to apprehend; so he made a short story of it, and resumed his walk, thankful that he had got rid of Tom.

Mr. Spicer and his friend, after fastening the horse to the fence, went to the woods in search of Tom.

Bobby reached the station just in time to take the cars, and in a moment was on his way to the city.

CHAPTER XV.

IN WHICH BOBBY GETS INTO A SCRAPE, AND TOM SPICER TURNS UP AGAIN.

Bobby had a poorer opinion of human nature than ever before. It seemed almost incredible to him that words so fairly spoken as those of Tom Spicer could be false. He had just risen from a sick bed, where he had had an opportunity for long and serious reflection. Tom had promised fairly, and Bobby had every reason to suppose he intended to be a good boy. But his promises had been lies. He had never intended to reform, at least not since he had got off his bed of pain. He was mortified and disheartened at the failure of this attempt to restore him to himself.

Like a great many older and wiser persons than himself, he was prone to judge the whole human family by a single individual. He did not come to believe that every man was a rascal, but, in more general terms, that there is a great deal more rascality in this world than one would be willing to believe.

With this sage reflection, he dismissed Tom from his mind, which very naturally turned again to the air castle which had been so ruthlessly upset. Then 'tis opinion of " the rest of mankind " was reversed; and he reflected that if the world were only peopled by angels like Annie Lee, what a pleasant place it would be to live in. She could not tell a lie, she could not use bad language, she could not steal, or do any thing else that was bad; and the prospect was decidedly pleasant. It was very agreeable to turn from Tom to Annie, and in a moment his air castle was built again, and throned on clouds of gold and purple. I do not know what impossible things he imagined, or how far up in the clouds he would have gone, if the arrival of the train at the city had not interrupted his thoughts, and pitched him down upon the earth again

Bobby was not one of that impracticable class of persons who do nothing but dream; for he felt that he had a mission to perform which dreaming could

not accomplish. However pleasant it may be to
think of the great and brilliant things which one *will*
do, to one of Bobby's practical character it was even
more pleasant to perform them. We all dream great
things, imagine great things ; but he who stops there
does not amount to much, and the world can well
spare him, for he is nothing but a drone in the hive.
Bobby's fine imaginings were pretty sure to bring out
a "now or never," which was the pledge of action,
and the work was as good as done when he had
said it.

Therefore, when the train arrived, Bobby did not
stop to dream any longer. He forgot his beautiful
air castle, and even let Annie Lee slip from his mind
for the time being. Those towns upon the Kennebec,
the two hundred books he was to sell, loomed up before him, for it was with them he had to do.

Grasping the little valise he carried with him, he
was hastening out of the station house when a hand
was placed upon his shoulder.

"Got off slick — didn't I?" said Tom Spicer, placing himself by Bobby's side.

"You here, Tom!" exclaimed our hero, gazing
with astonishment at his late companion.

It was not an agreeable encounter, and from the bottom of his heart Bobby wished him any where but where he was. He foresaw that he could not easily get rid of him.

"I am here," replied Tom. "I ran through the woods to the depot, and got aboard the cars just as they were starting. The old man couldn't come it over me quite so slick as that."

"But you ran away from home."

"Well, what of it?"

"A good deal, I should say."

"If you had been in my place, you would have done the same."

"I don't know about that; obedience to parents is one of our first duties."

"I know that; and if I had had any sort of fair play, I wouldn't have run away."

"What do you mean by that?" asked Bobby, somewhat surprised, though he had a faint idea of the meaning of the other.

"I will tell you all about it by and by. I give you my word and honor that I will make every thing satisfactory to you."

"But you lied to me on the road this morning"

Tom winced; under ordinary circumstances he would have resented such a remark by "clearing away" for a fight. But he had a purpose to accomplish, and he knew the character of him with whom he had to deal.

"I am sorry I did, now," answered Tom, with every manifestation of penitence for his fault. "I didn't want to lie to you; and it went against my conscience to do so. But I was afraid, if I told you my father refused, up and down, to let me go, that you wouldn't be willing I should come with you."

"I shall not be any more willing now I know all about it," added Bobby, in an uncompromising tone.

"Wait till you have heard my story, and then you won't blame me."

"Of course you can go where you please; it is none of my business; but let me tell you, Tom, in the beginning, that I won't go with a fellow who has run away from his father and mother."

"Pooh! What's the use of talking in that way?"

Tom was evidently disconcerted by this decided stand of his companion. He knew that his bump of firmness was well developed, and whatever he said he meant.

"You had better return home, Tom. Boys that run away from home don't often amount to much. Take my advice, and go home," added Bobby.

"To such a home as mine!" said Tom, gloomily. "If I had such a home as yours, I would not have left it."

Bobby got a further idea from this remark of the true state of the case, and the consideration moved him. Tom's father was a notoriously intemperate man, and the boy had nothing to hope for from his precept or his example. He was the child of a drunkard, and as much to be pitied as blamed for his vices. His home was not pleasant. He who presided over it, and who should have made a paradise of it, was its evil genius, a demon of wickedness, who blasted its flowers as fast as they bloomed.

Tom had seemed truly penitent both during his illness and since his recovery. His one great desire now was to get away from home, for home to him was a place of torment. Bobby suspected all this, and in his great heart he pitied his companion. He did not know what to do.

"I am sorry for you, Tom," said he, after he had considered the matter in this new light; "but I don't see what I can do for you. I doubt whether it would be right for me to help you run away from your parents."

"I don't want you to help me run away. I have done that already."

"But if I let you go with me, it will be just the same thing. Besides, since you told me those lies this morning, I haven't much confidence in you."

"I couldn't help that."

"Yes, you could. Couldn't help lying?"

"What could I do? You would have gone right back and told my father."

"Well, we will go up to Mr. Bayard's store, and then we will see what can be done."

"I couldn't stay at home, sure," continued Tom, as they walked along together. "My father even talked of binding me out to a trade."

"Did he?"

Bobby stopped short in the street; for it was evident that, as this would remove him from his unhappy home, and thus effect all he professed to desire, he had some other purpose in view.

"What are you stopping for, Bob?"

"I think you better go back, Tom."

"Not I; I won't do that, whatever happens."

"If your father will put you to a trade, what more do you want?"

'I won't go to a trade, any how."

Bobby said no more, but determined to consult with Mr. Bayard about the matter; and Tom was soon too busily engaged in observing the strange sights and sounds of the city to think of any thing else.

When they reached the store, Bobby went into Mr. Bayard's private office and told him all about the affair. The bookseller decided that Tom had run away more to avoid being bound to a trade than because his home was unpleasant; and this decision seemed to Bobby all the more just because he knew that Tom's mother, though a drunkard's wife, was a very good woman. Mr. Bayard further decided that Bobby ought not to permit the runaway to be the companion of his journey. He also considered it his duty to write to Mr. Spicer, informing him of his son's arrival in the city, and clearing Bobby from any agency in his escape.

While Mr. Bayard was writing the letter, Bobby went out to give Tom the result of the consultation. The runaway received it with a great show of emotion, and begged and pleaded to have the decision reversed. But Bobby, though he would gladly have done any thing for him which was consistent with his duty, was firm as a rock, and positively refused to have any thing to do with him until he obtained his father's consent; or, if there was any such trouble as he asserted, his mother's consent.

Tom left the store, apparently "more in sorrow than in anger." His bullying nature seemed to be cast out, and Bobby could not but feel sorry for him. Duty was imperative, as it always is, and it must be done "now or never."

During the day the little merchant attended to the packing of his stock, and to such other preparations as were required for his journey. He must take the steamer that evening for Bath, and when the time for his departure arrived, he was attended to the wharf by Mr. Bayard and Ellen, with whom he had passed the afternoon. The bookseller assisted him in procuring his ticket and berth, and gave him such instructions as his inexperience demanded.

The last bell rang, the fasts were cast off, and the great wheels of the steamer began to turn. Our hero, who had never been on the water in a steamboat, or indeed any thing bigger than a punt on the river at home, was much interested and excited by his novel position. He seated himself on the promenade deck, and watched with wonder the boiling, surging waters astern of the steamer.

How powerful is man, the author of that mighty machine that bore him so swiftly over the deep blue waters! Bobby was a little philosopher, as we have before had occasion to remark, and he was decidedly of the opinion that the steamboat was a great institution. When he had in some measure conquered his amazement, and the first ideas of sublimity which the steamer and the sea were calculated to excite in a poetical imagination, he walked forward to take a closer survey of the machinery After all, there was something rather comical in the affair. The steam hissed and sputtered, and the great walking beam kept flying up and down; and the sum total of Bobby's philosophy was, that it was funny these things should make the boat go so like a race horse over the water.

Then he took a look into the pilot house, and it seemed more funny that turning that big wheel should steer the boat. But the wind blew rather fresh at the forward part of the boat, and as Bobby's philosophy was not proof against it, he returned to the promenade deck, which was sheltered from the severity of the blast. He had got reconciled to the whole thing, and ceased to bother his head about the big wheel, the sputtering steam, and the walking beam; so he seated himself, and began to wonder what all the people in Riverdale were about.

"All them as hasn't paid their fare, please walk up to the cap'n's office and s-e-t-t-l-e!" shouted a colored boy, presenting himself just then, and furiously ringing a large hand bell.

"I have just settled," said Bobby, alluding to his comfortable seat.

But the illusion was so indefinite to the colored

boy that he thought himself insulted. He did not appear to be a very amiable boy, for his fist was doubled up, and with sundry big oaths, he threatened to annihilate the little merchant for his insolence.

"I didn't say any thing that need offend you," replied Bobby. "I meant nothing."

"You lie! You did!"

He was on the point of administering a blow with his fist, when a third party appeared on the ground, and without waiting to hear the merits of the case, struck the negro a blow which had nearly floored him.

Some of the passengers now interfered, and the colored boy was prevented from executing vengeance on the assailant.

"Strike that fellow and you strike me!" said he who had struck the blow.

"Tom Spicer!" exclaimed Bobby, astonished and chagrined at the presence of the runaway.

CHAPTER XVI.

IN WHICH BOBBY FINDS "IT IS AN ILL WIND THAT BLOWS NO ONE ANY GOOD."

A GENTLEMAN, who was sitting near Bobby when he made the remark which the colored boy had misunderstood, interfered to free him from blame, and probably all unpleasant feelings might have been saved, if Tom's zeal had been properly directed. As it was, the waiter retired with his bell, vowing vengeance upon his assailant.

"How came you here, Tom?" asked Bobby, when the excitement had subsided.

"You don't get rid of me so easily," replied Tom, laughing.

Bobby called to mind the old adage that "a bad penny is sure to return;" and, if it had not been a very uncivil remark, he would have said it.

"I didn't expect to see you again at present," he observed, hardly knowing what to say or do.

"I suppose not; but as I didn't mean you should expect me, I kept out of sight. Only for that darkey you wouldn't have found me out so soon. I like you, Bob, in spite of all you have done to get rid of me, and I wasn't a going to let the darkey thrash you."

"You only made matters worse."

"That is all the thanks I get for hitting him for you."

"I am sorry you hit him; at the same time I suppose you meant to do me a service, and I thank you, not for the blow you struck the black boy, but for your good intentions."

"That sounds better. I meant well, Bob."

"I dare say you did. But how came you here?"

"Why, you see, I was bound to go with you any how or at least to keep within hail of you. You told me, you know, that you were going in the steamboat; and after I left the shop, what should I see but a big picture of a steamboat on a wall. It said, 'Bath, Gardiner, and Hallowell,' on the bill; and I knew that was where you meant to go. So this afternoon I hunts round and finds the steamboat. I thought I never should have found it; but here I am."

"What are you going to do?"

"Going into the book business," replied Tom, with a smile.

"Where are your books?"

"Down stairs, in the cellar of the steamboat, or whatever you call it."

"Where did you get them?"

"Bought 'em, of course."

"Did you? Where?"

"Well, I don't remember the name of the street now. I could go right there if I was in the city, though."

"Would they trust you?"

Tom hesitated. The lies he had told that morning had done him no good — had rather injured his cause; and, though he had no principle that forbade lying, he questioned its policy in the present instance.

"I paid part down, and they trusted me part."

"How many books you got?"

"Twenty dollars worth. I paid eight dollars down."

"You did? Where did you get the eight dollars?"

Bobby remembered the money Tom's father had lost several weeks before, and immediately connected that circumstance with his present ability to pay so large a sum.

Tom hesitated again, but he was never at a loss for an answer.

"My mother gave it to me."

"Your mother?"

"Yes, *sir!*" replied Tom, boldly, and in that peculiarly bluff manner which is almost always good evidence that the boy is lying.

"But you ran away from home."

"That's so; but my mother knew I was coming."

"Did she?"

"To be sure she did."

"You didn't say so before."

"I can't tell all I know in a minute."

"If I thought your mother consented to your coming, I wouldn't say another word."

"Well, she did; you may bet your life on that."

"And your mother gave you ten dollars?"

"Who said she gave me *ten* dollars?" asked Tom a little sharply.

That was just the sum his father had lost, and Bobby had unwittingly hinted his suspicion.

"You must have had as much as that if you paid eight on your books. Your fare to Boston and your steamboat fare must be two dollars more."

"I know that; but look here, Bob;" and Tom took from his pocket five half dollars and exhibited them to his companion. "She gave me thirteen dollars."

Notwithstanding this argument, Bobby felt almost sure that the lost ten dollars was a part of his capital.

"I will tell you my story now, Bob, if you like. You condemned me without a hearing, as Jim Guthrie said when they sent him to the House of Correction for getting drunk."

"Go ahead."

The substance of Tom's story was, that his father drank so hard, and was such a tyrant in the house, that he could endure it no longer. His father and mother did not agree, as any one might have suspected. His mother, encouraged by the success of Bobby, thought that Tom might do something of the kind, and she had provided him the money to buy his ock of books

Bobby had not much confidence in this story. He had been deceived once; besides, it was not consistent with his previous narrative, and he had not before hinted that he had obtained his mother's consent. But Tom was eloquent, and protested that he had reformed. and meant to do well. He declared, by all that was good and great, Bobby should never have reason to be ashamed of him.

Our little merchant was troubled. He could not now get rid of Tom without actually quarrelling with him, or running away from him. He did not wish to do the former, and it was not an easy matter to do the latter. Besides, there was hope that the runaway would do well: and if he did, when he carried the profits of his trade home, his father would forgive him. One thing was certain; if he returned to Riverdale he would be what he had been before.

For these reasons Bobby finally, but very reluctantly, consented that Tom should remain with him, resolving, however, that, if he did not behave himself, he would leave him at once.

Before morning he had another reason. When the steamer got out into the open bay, Bobby was seasick. He retired to his berth with a dreadful headache, as he described it afterwards, it seemed just as though that great walking beam was smashing up and down right in the midst of his brains. He had never felt so ill before in his life, and was very sure, in his inexperience, that something worse than mere seasickness ailed him.

He told Tom, who was not in the least affected, how he felt; whereupon the runaway blustered round, got the steward and the captain into the cabin, and was very sure that Bobby would die before morning, if we may judge by the fuss he made.

The captain was angry at being called from the pilot house for nothing, and threatened to throw Tom overboard if he didn't stop his noise. The steward, however, was a kind-hearted man, and assured Bobby that passengers were often a great deal sicker than he was; but he promised to do something for his relief, and Tom went with him to his state room for the desired remedy.

The potion was nothing more nor less than a table spoonful of brandy, which Bobby, who had conscientious scruples about drinking ardent spirits, at first refused to take. Then Tom argued the point, and the sick boy yielded. The dose made him sicker yet, and nature came to his relief, and in a little while he felt better.

Tom behaved like a good nurse; he staid by his friend till he went to sleep, and then "turned in" upon a settee beneath his berth. The boat pitched and tumbled about so in the heavy sea that Bobby did not sleep long, and when he woke he found Tom ready to assist him. But our hero felt better, and entreated Tom to go to sleep again. He made the best of his unpleasant situation. Sleep was not to be wooed, and he tried to pass away the dreary hours in thinking of Riverdale and the dear ones there. His mother was asleep, and Annie was asleep; and that was about all the excitement he could get up even on the home question. He could not build castles in the air, for seasickness and castle building do not agree. The gold and purple clouds would be black in spite of him, and the aerial structure he essayed to build would pitch and tumble about, for all the world, just like a steamboat in a heavy sea. As often as he got fairly into it, he was violently roiled

out, and in a twinkling found himself in his narrow
berth, awfully seasick.

He went to sleep again at last, and the long nigh
passed away. When he woke in the morning, he felt
tolerably well, and was thankful that he had got out
of that scrape. But before he could dress himself, he
heard a terrible racket on deck. The steam whistle
was shrieking, the bell was banging, and he heard
the hoarse bellowing of the captain. It was certain
that something had happened, or was about to happen.

Then the boat stopped, rolling heavily in the sea.
Tom was not there; he had gone on deck. Bobby
was beginning to consider what a dreadful thing a
wreck was, when Tom appeared.

"What's the matter?" asked Bobby, with some
appearance of alarm.

"Fog," replied Tom. "It is so thick you can cut
with a hatchet."

"Is that all?"

"That's enough.'

"Where are we?"

"That is just what the pilot would like to know,

They can't see ahead a bit, and don't know where we are."

Bobby went on deck. The ocean rolled beneath them, but there was nothing but fog to be seen above and around them. The lead was heaved every few moments, and the steamer crept slowly along till it was found the water shoaled rapidly, when the captain ordered the men to let go the anchor.

There they were; the fog was as obstinate as a mule, and would not "lift." Hour after hour they waited, for the captain was a prudent man, and would not risk the life of those on board to save a few hours' time. After breakfast, the passengers began to display their uneasiness, and some of them called the captain very hard names, because he would not go on. Almost every body grumbled, and made themselves miserable.

"Nothing to do and nothing to read," growled a nicely-dressed gentleman, as he yawned and stretched himself to manifest his sensation of *ennui*.

"Nothing to read, eh?" thought Bobby. "We will soon supply that want."

Calling Tom, they went down to the main deck, where the baggage had been placed.

"Now's our time," said he, as he proceeded to unlock one of the trunks that contained his books. "Now or never."

"I am with you," replied Tom, catching the idea.

The books of the latter were in a box, and he was obliged to get a hammer to open it; but with Bobby's assistance he soon got at them.

"Buy 'The Wayfarer,'" said Bobby, when he returned to the saloon, and placed a volume in the hands of the yawning gentleman. "Best book of the season; only one dollar."

"That I will, and glad of the chance," replied the gentleman. "I would give five dollars for any thing, if it were only the 'Comic Almanac.'"

Others were of the same mind. There was no present prospect that the fog would lift, and before dinner time our merchant had sold fifty copies of "The Wayfarer." Tom, whose books were of an inferior description, and who was inexperienced as a salesman, disposed of twenty, which was more than half of his stock. The fog was a godsend to both of them, and they reaped a rich harvest from the occasion, for almost all the passengers seemed willing to spend their money freely for the means of occupying the heavy hours, and driving away that dreadful *ennui* which reigns supreme in a fog-bound steamer.

About the middle of the afternoon, the fog blew over, and the boat proceeded on her voyage, and before sunset our young merchants were safely landed at Bath.

CHAPTER XVII.

IN WHICH TOM HAS A GOOD TIME, AND BOBBY MEETS WITH A TERRIBLE MISFORTUNE.

BATH afforded our young merchants an excellent market for their wares, and they remained there the rest of the week. They then proceeded to Brunswick, where their success was equally flattering.

Thus far Tom had done very well, though Bobby had frequent occasion to remind him of the pledges he had given to conduct himself in a proper manner. He would swear now and then, from the force of habit; but invariably, when Bobby checked him, he promised to do better.

At Brunswick Tom sold the last of his books, and was in possession of about thirty dollars, twelve of which he owed the publisher who had furnished his stock. This money seemed to burn in his pocket. He had the means of having a good time, and it went hard with him to plod along as Bobby did, careful to save every penny he could.

"Come, Bob, let's get a horse and chaise and have a ride — what do you say?" proposed Tom, on the day he finished selling his books.

"I can't spare the time or the money," replied Bobby, decidedly.

"What is the use of having money if we can't spend it? It is a first rate day, and we should have a good time."

"I can't afford it. I have a great many books to sell."

"About a hundred; you can sell them fast enough."

"I don't spend my money foolishly."

"It wouldn't be foolishly. I have sold out, and I am bound to have a little fun now."

"You never will succeed if you do business in that way."

"Why not?"

"You will spend your money as fast as you get it."

"Pooh! we can get a horse and chaise for the afternoon for two dollars. That is not much."

"Considerable, I should say. But if you begin

there is no knowing where to leave off. I make it a rule not to spend a single cent foolishly, and if I don't begin, I shall never do it."

"I don't mean to spend all I get; only a little now and then," persisted Tom.

"Don't spend the first dollar for nonsense, and then you won't spend the second. Besides, when I have any money to spare, I mean to buy books with it for my library."

"Humbug! Your library!"

"Yes, my library; I mean to have a library one of these days."

"I don't want any library, and I mean to spend some of my money in having a good time; and if you won't go with me, I shall go alone — that's all."

"You can do as you please, of course; but I advise you to keep your money. You will want it to buy another stock of books."

"I shall have enough for that. What do you say? will you go with me or not?"

"No, I will not."

"Enough said; then I shall go alone, or get some fellow to go with me.'

"Consider well before you go," pleaded Bobby who had sense enough to see that Tom's proposed "good time" would put back, if not entirely prevent, the reform he was working out.

He then proceeded to reason with him in a very earnest and feeling manner, telling him he would not only spend all his money, but completely unfit himself for business. What he proposed to do was nothing more nor less than extravagance, and it would lead him to dissipation and ruin.

"To-day I am going to send one hundred dollars to Mr. Bayard," continued Bobby; "for I am afraid to have so much money with me. I advise you to send your money to your employer."

"Humph! Catch me doing that! I am bound to have a good time, any how."

"At least, send the money you owe him."

"I'll bet I won't."

"Well, do as you please; I have said all I have to say."

"You are a fool, Bob!" exclaimed Tom, who had evidently used Bobby as much as he wished, and no longer cared to speak soft words to him.

"Perhaps I am; but I know better than to spend my money upon fast horses. If you will go, I can't help it. I am sorry you are going astray."

"What do you mean by that, you young monkey?" said Tom, angrily.

This was Tom Spicer, the bully. It sounded like him; and with a feeling of sorrow Bobby resigned the hopes he had cherished of making a good boy of him.

"We had better part now," added our hero, sadly.

"I'm willing."

"I shall leave Brunswick this afternoon for the towns up the river. I hope no harm will befall you Good by, Tom."

"Go it! I have heard your preaching about long enough, and I am more glad to get rid of you than you are to get rid of me."

Bobby walked away towards the house where he had left the trunk containing his books, while Tom made his way towards a livery stable. The boys had been in the place for several days, and had made some acquaintances; so Tom had no difficulty in procuring a companion for his proposed ride.

Our hero wrote a letter that afternoon to Mr. Bayard, in which he narrated all the particulars of his journey, his relations with Tom Spicer, and the success that had attended his labors. At the bank he procured a hundred dollar note for his small bills, and enclosed it in the letter.

He felt sad about Tom. The runaway had done so well, had been so industrious, and shown such a tractable spirit, that he had been very much encouraged about him. But if he meant to be wild again, — for it was plain that the ride was only " the beginning of sorrows," — it was well that they should part.

By the afternoon stage our hero proceeded to Gardiner, passing through several smaller towns, which did not promise a very abundant harvest. His usual success attended him; for wherever he went, people seemed to be pleased with him, as Squire Lee had declared they would be. His pleasant, honest face was a capital recommendation, and his eloquence seldom failed to achieve the result which eloquence has ever achieved from Demosthenes down to the present day.

Our limits do not permit us to follow him in all his peregrinations from town to town, and from house to house; so we pass over the next fortnight, at the end of which time we find him at Augusta. He had sold all his books but twenty, and had that day remitted eighty dollars more to Mr. Bayard. It was Wednesday, and he hoped to sell out so as to be able to take the next steamer for Boston, which was advertised to sail on the following day.

He had heard nothing from Tom since their parting, and had given up all expectation of meeting him again; but that bad penny maxim proved true once more, for, as he was walking through one of the streets of Augusta, he had the misfortune to meet him — and this time it was indeed a misfortune.

"Hallo, Bobby!" shouted the runaway, as familiarly as though nothing had happened to disturb the harmony of their relations.

"Ah, Tom, I didn't expect to see you again," replied Bobby, not very much rejoiced to meet his late companion.

"I suppose not; but here I am, as good as new Have you sold out?"

"No, not quite."

"How many have you left?"

"About twenty; but I thought, Tom, you would have returned to Boston before this time."

"No;" and Tom did not seem to be in very good spirits.

"Where are you going now?"

"I don't know. I ought to have taken your advice, Bobby."

This was a concession, and our hero began to feel some sympathy for his companion — as who does not when the erring confess their faults?

"I am sorry you did not."

"I got in with some pretty hard fellows down there to Brunswick," continued Tom, rather sheepishly.

"And spent all your money," added Bobby, who could readily understand the reason why Tom had put on his humility again.

"Not all."

"How much have you left?"

"Not much," replied he, evasively. "I don't know what I shall do. I am in a strange place, and have no friends."

Bobby's sympathies were aroused, and withou

reflection, he promised to be a friend in his extremity.

"I will stick by you this time, Bob, come what will. I will do just as you say, now."

Our merchant was a little flattered by this unreserved display of confidence. He did not give weight enough to the fact that it was adversity alone which made Tom so humble. He was in trouble, and gave him all the guarantee he could ask for his future good behavior. He could not desert him now he was in difficulty.

"You shall help me sell my books, and then we will return to Boston together. Have you money enough left to pay your employer?"

Tom hesitated; something evidently hung heavily upon his mind.

"I don't know how it will be after I have paid my expenses to Boston," he replied, averting his face.

Bobby was perplexed by this evasive answer; but as Tom seemed so reluctant to go into details, he reserved his inquiries for a more convenient season.

"Now, Tom, you take the houses on that side of the street, and I will take those upon this side. You shall have the profits on all you sell"

"You are a first rate fellow, Bob; and I only wish I had done as you wanted me to do."

"Can't be helped now, and we will do the next best thing," replied Bobby, as he left his companion to enter a house.

Tom did very well, and by the middle of the afternoon they had sold all the books but four. "The Wayfarer" had been liberally advertised in that vicinity, and the work was in great demand. Bobby's heart grew lighter as the volumes disappeared from his valise, and already he had begun to picture the scene which would ensue upon his return to the little black house. How glad his mother would be to see him, and, he dared believe, how happy Annie would be as she listened to the account of his journey in the State of Maine! Wouldn't she be astonished when he told her about the steamboat, about the fog, and about the wild region at the mouth of the beautiful Kennebec!

Poor Bobby! the brightest dream often ends in sadness; and a greater trial than any he had been called upon to endure was yet in store for him

As he walked along, thinking of Riverdale and its

lo'ed ones, Tom came out of a grocery store where he
had just sold a book.

"Here, Bob, is a ten dollar bill. I believe I have
sold ten books for you," said Tom, after they had
walked some distance. "You had better keep the
money now; and while I think of it, you had better
take what I have left of my former sales;" and Tom
handed him another ten dollar bill.

Bobby noticed that Tom seemed very much confused and embarrassed; but he did not observe that the two bills he had handed him were on the same bank.

"Then you had ten dollars left after your frolic,"
he remarked, as he took the last bill.

"About that;" and Tom glanced uneasily behind
him.

"What is the matter with you, Tom?" asked
Bobby, who did not know what to make of his companion's embarrassment.

"Nothing, Bob; let us walk a little faster. We
had better turn up this street," continued Tom, as,
with a quick pace, he took the direction indicated.

Bobby began to fear that Tom had been doing

something wrong; and the suspicion was confirmed by seeing two men running with all their might towards them. Tom perceived them at the same moment.

"Run!" he shouted, and suiting the action to the word, he took to his heels, and fled up the street into which he had proposed to turn.

Bobby did not run, but stopped short where he was till the men came up to him.

"Grab him," said one of them, "and I will catch the other."

The man collared Bobby, and in spite of all the resistance he could make, dragged him down the street to the grocery store in which Tom had sold his last book.

"What do you mean by this?" asked Bobby, his blood boiling with indignation at the harsh treatment to which he had been subjected.

"We have got you, my hearty," replied the man, releasing his hold.

No sooner was the grasp of the man removed, than Bobby, who determined on this as on former occasions to stand upon his inalienable rights, bolted for the door, and ran away with all his speed. But his captor was too fleet for him, and he was immediately retaken. To make him sure this time, his arms were tied behind him, and he was secured to the counter of the shop.

In a few moments the other man returned dragging Tom in triumph after him. By this time quite a crowd had collected, which nearly filled the store.

Bobby was confounded at the sudden change that had come over his fortunes; but seeing that resistance would be vain, he resolved to submit with the best grace he could.

" I should like to know what all this means?" he inquired, indignantly.

The crowd laughed in derision.

" This is the chap that stole the wallet, I will be bound," said one, pointing to Tom, who stood in surly silence awaiting his fate.

" He is the one who came into the store," replied the shopkeeper.

"*I* haven't stole any wallet," protested Bobby, who now understood the whole affair.

The names of the two boys were taken, and warrants procured for their detention. They were searched, and upon Tom was found the lost wallet, and upon Bobby two ten dollar bills, which the loser was willing to swear had been in the wallet. The evidence therefore was conclusive, and they were both sent to jail.

Poor Bobby! the inmate of a prison!

The law took its course, and in due time both of them were sentenced to two years' imprisonment in the State Reform School. Bobby was innocent, but he could not make his innocence appear. He had been the companion of Tom, the real thief, and part of the money had been found upon his person. Tom was too mean to exonerate him, and even had the hardihood to exult over his misfortune.

At the end of three days they reached the town in which the Reform School is located, and were duly committed for their long term.

Poor Bobby!

CHAPTER XVIII.

IN WHICH BOBBY TAKES FRENCH LEAVE, AND CAMPS IN THE WOODS.

THE intelligence of Bobby's misfortune reached Mr. Bayard, in Boston, by means of the newspapers. To the country press an item is a matter of considerable importance, and the alleged offence against the peace and dignity of the State of Maine was duly heralded to the inquiring public as a "daring robbery." The reporter who furnished the facts in the case for publication was not entirely devoid of that essential qualification of the country item writer, a lively imagination, and was obliged to dress up the particulars a little, in order to produce the necessary amount of wonder and indignation. It was stated that one of the two young men had been prowling about the place for several days, ostensibly for the purpose of selling books, but really with the intention of stealing whatever he could lay his hands upon. It was suggested that the boys were in league with an organized band of robbers, whose nefarious purposes would be defeated by the timely arrest of these young villains. The paper hinted that further depredations would probably be discovered, and warned people to beware of ruffians strolling about the country in the guise of pedlers.

The writer of this thrilling paragraph must have had reason to believe that he had discharged his whole duty to the public, and that our hero was duly branded as a desperate fellow. No doubt he believed Bobby was an awful monster; for at the conclusion of his remarks he introduced some severe strictures on the lenity of the magistrate, because he had made the sentence two years, instead of five, which the writer thought the atrocious crime deserved. But, then, the justice differed from him in politics, which may account for the severity of the article.

Mr. Bayard read this precious paragraph with mingled grief and indignation. He understood the case at a glance. Tom Spicer had joined him, and the little merchant had been involved in his crime. He was sure that Bobby had had no part in stealing the money. One so noble and true as he had been could not steal, he reasoned. It was contrary to experience, contrary to common sense.

He was very much disturbed. This intelligence would be a severe blow to the poor boy's mother, and he had not the courage to destroy all her bright hopes by writing her the terrible truth. He was confident that Bobby was innocent, and that his being in the company of Tom Spicer had brought the imputation upon him; so he could not let the matter take its course. He was determined to do something to procure his liberty and restore his reputation.

Squire Lee was in the city that day, and had left his store only half an hour before he discovered the paragraph. He immediately sent to his hotel for him, and together they devised means to effect Bobby's liberation. The squire was even more confident than Mr. Bayard that our hero was innocent of the crime charged upon him. They agreed to proceed immediately to the State of Maine, and use their influence in obtaining his pardon. The bookseller was a man of influence in the community, and was as well known in Maine as in Massachusetts; but to make their application the surer, he procured letters of introduction from some of the most distinguished men in Boston to the governor and other official persons in Maine.

We will leave them now to do the work they had so generously undertaken, and return to the Reform School, where Bobby and Tom were confined. The latter took the matter very coolly. He seemed to feel that he deserved his sentence, but he took a malicious delight in seeing Bobby the companion of his captivity. He even had the hardihood to remind him of the blow he had struck him more than two months before, telling him that he had vowed vengeance then, and now the time had come. He was satisfied.

"You know I didn't steal the money, or have any thing to do with it," said Bobby.

"Some of it was found upon you, though," sneered Tom, maliciously.

"You know how it came there, if no one else does."

"Of course I do; but I like your company too well to get rid of you so easy."

"The Lord is with the innocent," replied Bobby; "and something tells me that I shall not stay in this place a great while."

"Going to run away?" asked Tom, with interest, and suddenly dropping his malicious look.

"I know I am innocent of any crime; and I know that the Lord will not let me stay here a great while."

"What do you mean to do, Bob?"

Bobby made no reply; he felt that he had had more confidence in Tom than he deserved, and he determined to keep his own counsel in future. He had a purpose in view. His innocence gave him courage; and perhaps he did not feel that sense of necessity for submission to the laws of the land which age and experience give. He prayed earnestly for deliverance from the place in which he was confined. He felt that he did not deserve to be there; and though it was a very comfortable place, and the boys fared as well as he wished to fare, still it seemed to him like a prison. He was unjustly detained; and he not only prayed to be delivered, but he resolved to work out his own deliverance at the first opportunity.

Knowing that whatever he had would be taken from him, he resolved by some means to keep possession of the twenty dollars he had about him. He had always kept his money in a secret place in his jacket to guard against accident, and the officers who had searched him had not discovered it. But now his clothes would be changed. He thought of these things before his arrival; so, when he reached the entrance, and got out of the wagon, to open the gate, by order of the officer, he slipped his twenty dollars into a hole in the wall.

It so happened that there was not a suit of clothes in the store room of the institution which would fit him; and he was permitted to wear his own dress till another should be made. After his name and description had been entered, and the superintendent had read him a lecture upon his future duties, he was permitted to join the other boys, who were at work on the farm. He was sent with half a dozen others to pick up stones in a neighboring field. No officer was with them, and Bobby was struck with the apparent freedom of the institution, and he so expressed himself to his companions.

"Not so much freedom as you think for," said one, in reply.

"I should think the fellows would clear out."

"Not so easy a matter. There is a standing reward of five dollars to any one who brings back a runaway."

"They must catch him first."

"No fellow ever got away yet. They always caught him before he got ten miles from the place."

This was an important suggestion to Bobby, who already had a definite purpose in his mind. Like a skilful general, he had surveyed the ground on his arrival, and was at once prepared to execute his design.

In his conversation with the boys, he obtained the history of several who had attempted to escape, and found that even those who got a fair start were taken on some public road. He perceived that they were not good generals, and he determined to profit by their mistake.

A short distance from the institution was what appeared to be a very extensive wood. Beyond this, many miles distant, he could see the ocean glittering like a sheet of ice under the setting sun.

He carefully observed the hills, and obtained the bearings of various prominent objects in the vicinity which would aid him in his flight. The boys gave him all the information in their power about the localities of the country. They seemed to feel that he was possessed of a superior spirit, and that he would not long remain among them; but, whatever they thought, they kept their own counsel

Bobby behaved well, and was so intelligent and prompt that he obtained the confidence of the superintendent, who began to employ him about the house, and in his own family. He was sent of errands in the neighborhood, and conducted himself so much to the satisfaction of his guardians that he was not required to work in the field after the second day of his residence on the farm.

One afternoon he was told that his clothes were ready, and that he might put them on the next morning. This was a disagreeable announcement; for Bobby saw that, with the uniform of the institution upon his back, his chance of escape would be very slight. But about sunset, he was sent by the superintendent's lady to deliver a note at a house in the vicinity.

"Now or never!" said Bobby to himself, after he had left the house. "Now's my time."

As he passed the gate, he secured his money, and placed it in the secret receptacle of his jacket. After he had delivered the letter, he took the road and hastened off in the direction of the wood. His heart beat wildly at the prospect of once more meeting his mother, after nearly four weeks' absence. Annie Lee would welcome him; she would not believe that he was a thief.

He had been four days an inmate of the Reform School, and nothing but the hope of soon attaining his liberty had kept his spirits from drooping. He had not for a moment despaired of getting away.

He reached the entrance to the wood, and taking a cart path, began to penetrate its hidden depths. The night darkened upon him; he heard the owl screech his dismal note, and the whip-poor-will chant his cheery song. A certain sense of security now pervaded his mind, for the darkness concealed him from the world, and he had placed six good miles between him and the prison, as he considered it.

He walked on, however, till he came to what

seemed to be the end of the wood, and he hoped to reach the blue ocean he had seen in the distance before morning. Leaving the forest, he emerged into the open country. There was here and there a house before him; but the aspect of the country seemed strangely familiar to him. He could not understand it. He had never been in this part of the country before; yet there was a great house with two barns by the side of it, which he was positive he had seen before.

He walked across the field a little farther, when, to his astonishment and dismay, he beheld the lofty turrets of the State Reform School. He had been walking in a circle, and had come out of the forest near the place where he had entered it.

Bobby, as the reader has found out by this time, was a philosopher as well as a hero; and instead of despairing or wasting his precious time in vain regrets at his mistake, he laughed a little to himself at the blunder, and turned back into the woods again.

"Now or never!" muttered he. "It will never do to give it up so."

For an hour he walked on, with his eyes fixed on

a great bright star in the sky. Then he found that the cart path crooked round, and he discovered where he had made his blunder. Leaving the road, he made his way in a straight line, still guided by the star, till he came to a large sheet of water.

The sheet of water was an effectual barrier to his farther progress; indeed, he was so tired he did not feel able to walk any more. He deemed himself safe from immediate pursuit in this secluded place. He needed rest, and he foresaw that the next few days would be burdened with fatigue and hardship which he must be prepared to meet.

Bobby was not nice about trifles, and his habits were such that he had no fear of taking cold. His comfortable bed in the little black house was preferable to the cold ground, even with the primeval forest for a chamber; but circumstances alter cases, and he did not waste any vain regrets about the necessity of his position. After finding a secluded spot in the wood, he raked the dry leaves together for a bed, and offering his simple but fervent prayer to the Great Guardian above, he lay down to rest. The owl screamed his dismal note, and the whip-poor-will still repeated his monotonous song; but they were good company in the solitude of the dark forest.

He could not go to sleep for a time, so strange and exciting were the circumstances of his position. He thought of a thousand things, but he could not *think* himself to sleep, as he was wont to do. At last nature, worn out by fatigue and anxiety, conquered the circumstances, and he slept.

CHAPTER XIX.

IN WHICH BOBBY HAS A NARROW ESCAPE, AND GOES TO SEA WITH SAM RAY.

NATURE was kind to the little pilgrim in his extremity, and kept his senses sealed in grateful slumber till the birds had sung their matin song, and the sun had risen high in the heavens.

Bobby woke with a start, and sprang to his feet. For a moment he did not realize where he was, or remember the exciting incidents of the previous evening. He felt refreshed by his deep slumber, and came out of it as vigorous as though he had slept in his bed at home. Rubbing his eyes, he stared about him at the tall pines whose foliage canopied his bed, and his identity was soon restored to him. He was Bobby Bright — but Bobby Bright in trouble. He was not the little merchant, but the little fugitive fleeing from the prison to which he had been doomed

It did not take him long to make his toilet, which was the only advantage of his primitive style of lodging. His first object was to examine his position, and ascertain in what direction he should continue his flight. He could not go ahead, as he had intended, for the sheet of water was an impassable barrier. Leaving the dense forest, he came to a marsh, beyond which was the wide creek he had seen in the night. It was salt water, and he reasoned that it could not extend a great way inland. His only course was to follow it till he found means of crossing it.

Following the direction of the creek, he kept near the margin of the wood till he came to a public road. He had some doubts about trusting himself out of the forest, even for a single moment; so he seated himself upon a rock to argue the point. If any one should happen to come along, he was almost sure of furnishing a clew to his future movements, if not of being immediately captured.

This was a very strong argument, but there was a stronger one upon the other side. He had eaten nothing since dinner on the preceding day, and he began to feel faint for the want of food. On the

other side of the creek he saw a pasture which looked
as though it might afford him a few berries; and he
was on the point of taking to the road, when he heard
the rumbling of a wagon in the distance.

His heart beat with apprehension. Perhaps it was
some officer of the institution in search of him. At
any rate it was some one who had come from the
vicinity of the Reform School, and who had probably
heard of his escape. As it came nearer, he heard the
jingling of bells; it was the baker. How he longed
for a loaf of his bread, or some of the precious gingerbread he carried in his cart! Hunger tempted him
to run the risk of exposure. He had money; he
could buy cakes and bread; and perhaps the baker had
a kind heart, and would befriend him in his distress.
The wagon was close at hand.

"Now or never," thought he; but this time it was
not *now*. The risk was too great. If he failed now,
two years of captivity were before him; and as for
the hunger, he could grin and bear it for a while.

"Now or never;" but this time it was escape now
or never; and he permitted the baker to pass without
hailing him.

He waited half an hour, and then determined to take the road till he had crossed the creek. The danger was great, but the pangs of hunger urged him on. He was sure there were berries in the pasture, and with a timid step, carefully watching before and behind to insure himself against surprise, he crossed the bridge. But then a new difficulty presented itself. There was a house within ten rods of the bridge, which he must pass, and to do so would expose him to the most imminent peril. He was on the point of retreating, when a man came out of the house, and approached him. What should he do? It was a trying moment. If he ran, the act would expose him to suspicion. If he went forward, the man might have already received a description of him, and arrest him.

He chose the latter course. The instinct of his being was to do every thing in a straightforward manner, and this probably prompted his decision.

"Good morning, sir," said he boldly to the man.

"Good morning. Where are you travelling?"

This was a hard question. He did not know where he was travelling; besides, even in his present difficult position, he could not readily resort to a lie.

"Down here a piece," he replied.

"Travelled far to-day?"

"Not far. Good morning, sir;" and Bobby resumed his walk.

"I say, boy, suppose you tell me where you are going;" and the man came close to him, and deliberately surveyed him from head to foot.

"I can hardly tell you," replied Bobby, summoning courage for the occasion.

"Well, I suppose not," added the man, with a meaning smile.

Bobby felt his strength desert him as he realized that he was suspected of being a runaway from the Reform School. That smile on the man's face was the knell of hope; and for a moment he felt a flood of misery roll over his soul. But the natural elasticity of his spirits soon came to his relief, and he resolved not to give up the ship, even if he had to fight for it.

"I am in a hurry, so I shall have to leave you."

"Not just yet, young man. Perhaps, as you don't know where you are going, you may remember what your name is,' continued the man, good naturedly.

There was a temptation to give a false name; but as it was so strongly beaten into our hero that the truth is better than a falsehood, he held his peace.

"Excuse me, sir, but I can't stop to talk now."

"In a hurry? Well, I dare say you are. I suppose there is no doubt but you are Master Robert Bright."

"Not the least, sir; I haven't denied it yet, and I am not ashamed of my name," replied Bobby, with a good deal of spirit.

"That's honest; I like that."

"'Honesty is the best policy,'" added Bobby.

"That's cool for a rogue, any how. You ought to thought of that afore."

"I did."

"And stole the money?"

"I didn't. I never stole a penny in my life."

"Come, I like that."

"It is the truth."

"But they won't believe it over to the Reform School," laughed the man.

"They will one of these days, perhaps."

"You are a smart youngster; but I don't know as

I can make five dollars any easier than by taking you back where you come from."

"Yes, you can," replied Bobby, promptly

"Can I?"

"Yes."

"How?"

"By letting me go."

"Eh; you talk flush. I suppose you mean to give me your note, payable when the Kennebec dries up."

"Cash on the nail," replied Bobby. "You look like a man with a heart in your bosom."— Bobby stole this passage from "The Wayfarer."

"I reckon I have. The time hasn't come yet when Sam Ray could see a fellow-creature in distress and not help him out. But to help a thief off——"

"We will argue that matter," interposed Bobby. "I can prove to you beyond a doubt that I am innocent of the crime charged upon me."

"You don't look like a bad boy, I must say."

"But, Mr. Ray, I'm hungry; I haven't eaten a mouthful since yesterday noon."

"Thunder! You don't say so!" exclaimed Sam Ray "I never could bear to see a man hungry, much more a boy; so come along to my house and get something to eat, and we will talk about the other matter afterwards."

Sam Ray took Bobby to the little old house in which he dwelt; and in a short time his wife, who expressed her sympathy for the little fugitive in the warmest terms, had placed an abundant repast upon the table. Our hero did ample justice to it, and when he had finished he felt like a new creature.

"Now, Mr. Ray, let me tell you my story." said Bobby.

"I don't know as it's any use. Now you have eat my bread and butter, I don't feel like being mean to you. If any body else wants to carry you back, they may; I won't."

"But you shall hear me;" and Bobby proceeded to deliver his "plain, unvarnished tale."

When he had progressed but a little way in the narrative, the noise of an approaching vehicle was heard. Sam looked out of the window, as almost every body does in the country when a carriage passes.

"By thunder! It's the Reform School wagon!" exclaimed he. "This way, boy!" and the good nparted man thrust him into his chamber, bidd'ı g him get under the bed.

The carriage stopped at the house; but Sam evaded a direct reply, and the superintendent — for it was he — proceeded on his search.

"Heaven bless you, Mr. Ray!" exclaimed Bobby, when he came out of the chamber, as the tears of gratitude coursed down his cheeks.

"O, you will find Sam Ray all right," said he, warmly pressing Bobby's proffered hand. "I ain't quite a heathen, though some folks around here think so."

"You are an angel!"

"Not exactly," laughed Sam.

Our hero finished his story, and confirmed it by exhibiting his account book and some other papers which he had retained. Sam Ray was satisfied, and vowed that if ever he saw Tom Spicer he would certainly "lick" him for his sake.

"Now, sonny, I like you; I will be sworn you are a good fellow; and I mean to help you off. So just come along with me. I make my living by browsing round, hunting and fishing a little, and doing an odd 'ob now and then. You see, I have got a good boat down the creek, and I shall just put you aboard and take you any where you have a mind to go."

"May Heaven reward you!" cried Bobby, almost overcome by this sudden and unexpected kindness.

"O, I don't want no reward; only when you get to be a great man — and I am dead sure you will be a great man — just think now and then of Sam Ray, and it's all right."

"I shall remember you with gratitude as long as I live."

Sam Ray took his gun on his shoulder, and Bobby the box of provision which Mrs. Ray had put up, and they left the house. At the bridge they got into a little skiff, and Sam took the oars. After they had passed a bend in the creek which concealed them from the road, Bobby felt secure from further molestation.

Sam pulled about two miles down the creek, where it widened into a broad bay, near the head of which was anchored a small schooner.

"Now, my hearty, nothing short of Uncle Sam's whole navy can get you away from me," said Sam, as he pulled alongside the schooner.

"You have been very kind to me."

"All right, sonny. Now tumble aboard."

Bobby jumped upon the deck of the little craft and Sam followed him, after making fast the skiff to the schooner's moorings.

In a few minutes the little vessel was standing down the bay with "a fresh wind and a flowing sheet." Bobby, who had never been in a sail boat before, was delighted, and in no measured terms expressed his admiration of the working of the trim little craft.

"Now, sonny, where shall we go?" asked Sam, as they emerged from the bay into the broad ocean.

"I don't know," replied Bobby. "I want to get back to Boston."

"Perhaps I can put you aboard of some coaster bound there."

"That will do nicely."

"I will head towards Boston, and if I don't over- haul any thing, I will take you there myself."

"Is this boat big enough to go so far?"

"She'll stand any thing short of a West India hur- ricane. You ain't afeerd, are you?"

"O, no; I like it."

The big waves now tossed the little vessel up and down like a feather, and the huge seas broke upon the bow, deluging her deck with floods of water. Bobby had unlimited confidence in Sam Ray, and felt as much at home as though he had been " cradled upon the briny deep." There was an excitement in the scene which accorded with his nature, and the perils which he had so painfully pictured on the preceding night were all born into the most lively joys.

They ate their dinners from the provision box; Sam lighted his pipe, and many a tale he told of adventure by sea and land. Bobby felt happy, and almost dreaded the idea of parting with his rough but goodhearted friend They were now far out at sea, and the night was coming on.

" Now, sonny, you had better turn in and take a snooze; you didn't rest much last night."

" I am not sleepy; but there is one thing I will do;" and Bobby drew from his secret receptacle his roll of bills.

" Put them up, sonny," said Sam.

" I want to make you a present of ten dollars."

" You can't do it."

"Nay, but to please me."

"No, sir!"

"Well, then, let me send it to your good wife."

"You can't do that, nuther," replied Sam, gazing earnestly at a lumber-laden schooner ahead of him.

"You must; your good heart made you lose five dollars, and I insist upon making it up to you."

"You can't do it."

"I shall feel bad if you don't take it. You see I have twenty dollars here, and I would like to give you the whole of it."

"Not a cent, sonny. I ain't a heathen. That schooner ahead is bound for Boston, I reckon."

"I shall be sorry to part with you, Mr. Rav."

"Just my sentiment. I hain't seen a youngster afore for many a day that I took a fancy to, and I hate to let you go."

"We shall meet again."

"I hope so."

"Please to take this money."

"No;" and Sam shook his head so resolutely that Bobby gave up the point.

As Sam had conjectured, the lumber schooner was

bound to Boston. Her captain readily agreed to take our hero on board, and he sadly bade adieu to his kind friend.

"Good by, Mr. Ray," said Bobby, as the schooner filled away. "Take this to remember me by."

It was his jackknife; but Sam did not discover the ten dollar bill, which was shut beneath the blade, till it was too late to return it.

Bobby did not cease to wave his hat to Sam till his little craft disappeared in the darkness.

CHAPTER XX.

IN WHICH THE CLOUDS BLOW OVER, AND BOBBY IS HIMSELF AGAIN.

FORTUNATELY for Bobby, the wind began to blow very heavily soon after he went on board of the lumber schooner, so that the captain was too much engaged in working his vessel to ask many questions. He was short handed, and though our hero was not much of a sailor he made himself useful to the best of his ability. Though the wind was heavy, it was not fair; and it was not till the third morning after his parting with Sam Ray that the schooner arrived off Boston Light. The captain then informed him that, as the tide did not favor him, he might not get up to the city for twenty-four hours; and, if he was in a hurry, he would put him on board a pilot boat which he saw standing up the channel.

"Thank you, captain; you are very kind, but

it would give you a great deal of trouble," said Bobby.

"None at all. We must wait here till the tide turns; so we have nothing better to do."

"I should be very glad to get up this morning."

"You shall, then;" and the captain ordered two men to get out the jolly boat.

"I will pay my passage now if you please."

"That is paid."

"Paid?"

"I should say you had worked your passage. You have done very well, and I shall not charge you any thing."

"I expected to pay my passage, captain; but if you think I have done enough to pay it, why I have nothing to say, only that I am very much obliged to you."

"You ought to be a sailor, young man; you were cut out for one."

"I like the sea, though I never saw it till a few weeks since. But I suppose my mother would not let me go to sea."

"I suppose not mothers are always afraid of salt water."

By this time the jolly boat was alongside; and bidding the captain adieu, he jumped into it, and the men pulled him to the pilot boat, which had come up into the wind at the captain's hail. Bobby was kindly received on board, and in a couple of hours landed at the wharf in Boston.

With a beating heart he made his way up into Washington Street. He felt strangely; his cheeks seemed to tingle, for he was aware that the imputation of dishonesty was fastened upon him. He could not doubt but that the story of his alleged crime had reached the city, and perhaps gone to his friends in Riverdale. How his poor mother must have wept to think her son was a thief! No; she never could have thought that. *She* knew he would not steal, if no one else did. And Annie Lee — would she ever smile upon him again? Would she welcome him to her father's house so gladly as she had done in the past? He could bring nothing to establish his innocence but his previous character. Would not Mr. Bayard frown upon him? Would not even Ellen be tempted to forget the service he had rendered her?

Bobby had thought of all these things before — on

his cold, damp bed in the forest, in the watches of the tempestuous night on board the schooner. But now, when he was almost in the presence of those he loved and respected, they had more force, and they nearly overwhelmed him.

"I am innocent," he repeated to himself, "and why need I fear? My good Father in heaven will not let me be wronged."

Yet he could not overcome his anxiety; and when he reached the store of Mr. Bayard, he passed by, dreading to face the friend who had been so kind to him. He could not bear even to be suspected of a crime by him.

"Now or never," said he, as he turned round. "I will know my fate at once, and then make the best of it."

Mustering all his courage, he entered the store. Mr. Timmins was not there; so he was spared the infliction of any ill-natured remark from him.

"Hallo, Bobby!" exclaimed the gentlemanly salesman, whose acquaintance he had made on his first visit.

"Good morning, Mr. Bigelow," replied Bobby with as much boldness as he could command

"I didn't know as I should ever see you again. You have been gone a long while."

"Longer than usual," answered Bobby, with a blush; for he considered the remark of the salesman as an allusion to his imprisonment. "Is Mr. Bayard in?"

"He is — in his office."

Bobby's feet would hardly obey the mandate of his will, and with a faltering step he entered the private room of the bookseller. Mr. Bayard was absorbed in the perusal of the morning paper, and did not observe his entrance. With his heart up in his throat, and almost choking him, he stood for several minutes upon the threshold. He almost feared to speak, dreading the severe frown with which he expected to be received. Suspense, however, was more painful than condemnation, and he brought his resolution up to the point.

"Mr. Bayard," said he, in faltering tones.

"Bobby!" exclaimed the bookseller, dropping his paper upon the floor, and jumping upon his feet as though an electric current had passed through his frame.

Grasping our hero's hand, he shook it with so much energy that, under any other circumstances, Bobby would have thought it hurt him. He did not think so now.

"My poor Bobby! I am delighted to see you!" continued Mr. Bayard.

Bobby burst into tears, and sobbed like a child, as he was. The unexpected kindness of this reception completely overwhelmed him.

"Don't cry, Bobby; I know all about it;" and the tender-hearted bookseller wiped away his tears. "It was a stroke of misfortune; but it is all right now."

But Bobby could not help crying, and the more Mr. Bayard attempted to console him, the more he wept.

"I am innocent, Mr. Bayard," he sobbed.

"I know you are, Bobby; and all the world knows you are."

"I am ruined now; I shall never dare to hold my head up again."

"Nonsense, Bobby; you will hold your head the higher. You have behaved like a hero."

"I ran away from the State Reform School, sir

I was innocent, and I would rather have died than staid there."

"I know all about it, my young friend. Now dry your tears, and we will talk it all over."

Bobby blowed and sputtered a little more; but finally he composed himself, and took a chair by Mr. Bayard's side. The bookseller then drew from his pocket a ponderous document, with a big official seal upon it, and exhibited it to our hero.

"Do you see this, Bobby? It is your free and unconditional pardon."

"Sir! Why——"

"It will all end well, you may depend."

Bobby was amazed. His pardon? But it would not restore his former good name. He felt that he was branded as a felon. It was not mercy, but justice, that he wanted.

"Truth is mighty, and will prevail," continued Mr. Bayard; "and this document restores your reputation."

"I can hardly believe that."

"Can't you? Hear my story then. When I read in one of the Maine papers the account of your misfortune, I felt that you had been grossly wronged

You were coupled with that Tom Spicer, who is the most consummate little villain I ever saw, and I understood your situation. Ah, Bobby, your only mistake was in having any thing to do with that fellow."

"I left him at Brunswick because he began to behave badly; but he joined me again at Augusta. He had spent nearly all his money, and did not know what to do. I pitied him, and meant to do something to help him out of the scrape."

"Generous as ever! I have heard all about this before."

"Indeed; who told you?"

"Tom Spicer himself."

"Tom?" asked Bobby, completely mystified.

"Yes, Tom; you see, when I heard about your trouble, Squire Lee and myself——"

"Squire Lee? Does he know about it?"

"He does; and you may depend upon it, he thinks more highly of you than ever before. He and I immediately went down to Augusta to inquire into the matter. We called upon the governor of the state, who said that he had seen you, and bought a book of you."

"Of me!" exclaimed Bobby, startled to think he had sold a book to a governor.

"Yes; you called at his house; probably you did not know that he was the chief magistrate of the state. At any rate, he was very much pleased with you, and sorry to hear of your misfortune. Well, we followed your route to Brunswick, where we ascertained how Tom had conducted. In a week he established a very bad reputation there; but nothing could be found to implicate you. The squire testified to your uniform good behavior, and especially to your devotion to your mother. In short, we procured your pardon, and hastened with it to the State Reform School.

"On our arrival, we learned, to our surprise and regret, that you had escaped from the institution on the preceding evening. Every effort was made to retake you, but without success. Ah, Bobby, you managed that well."

"They didn't look in the right place," replied Bobby, with a smile, for he began to feel happy again.

"By the permission of the superintendent, Squire

Lee and myself examined Tom Spicer. He is a great rascal. Perhaps he thought we would get him out; so he made a clean breast of it, and confessed that you had no hand in the robbery, and that you knew nothing about it. He gave you the two bills on purpose to implicate you in the crime. We wrote down his statement, and had it sworn to before a justice of the peace. You shall read it by and by."

"May Heaven reward you for your kindness to a poor boy!" exclaimed Bobby, the tears flowing down his cheeks again. "I did not deserve so much from you, Mr. Bayard."

"Yes, you did, and a thousand times more. I was very sorry you had left the institution, and I waited in the vicinity till they said there was no probability that you would be captured. The most extraordinary efforts were used to find you; but there was not a person to be found who had seen or heard of you. I was very much alarmed about you, and offered a hundred dollars for any information concerning you."

"I am sorry you had so much trouble. I wish I had known you were there."

"How did you get off?"

Bobby briefly related the story of his escape, and Mr. Bayard pronounced his skill worthy of his genius.

"Sam Ray is a good fellow; we will remember him," added the bookseller, when he had finished.

"I shall remember him; and only that I shall be afraid to go into the State of Maine after what has happened, I should pay him a visit one of these days."

"There you are wrong. Those who know your story would sooner think of giving you a public reception, than of saying or doing any thing to injure your feelings. Those who have suffered unjustly are always lionized."

"But no one will know my story, only that I was sent to prison for stealing."

"There you are mistaken again. We put articles in all the principal papers, stating the facts in tne case, and establishing your innocence beyond a peradventure Go to Augusta now, Bobby, and you will be a lion."

"I am sure I had no idea of getting out of the scrape so easily as this."

"Innocence shall triumph, my young friend."

"What does mother say?" asked Bobby, his countenance growing sad.

"I do not know. We returned from Maine only yesterday; but Squire Lee will satisfy her. All that can worry her, as it has worried me, will be her fears for your safety when she hears of your escape."

"I will soon set her mind at ease upon that point. I will take the noon train home."

"A word about business before you go. I discharged Timmins about a week ago, and I have kept his place for you."

"By gracious!" exclaimed Bobby, thrown completely out of his propriety by this announcement.

"I think you will do better, in the long run, than you would to travel about the country. I was talking with Ellen about it, and she says it shall be so. Timmins's salary was five hundred dollars a year, and you shall have the same."

"Five hundred dollars a year!" ejaculated Bobby, amazed at the vastness of the sum.

"Very well for a boy of thirteen, Bobby."

"I was fourteen last Sunday, sir."

"I would not give any other boy so much; but you are worth it, and you shall have it."

Probably Mr. Bayard's gratitude had something to do with this munificent offer; but he knew that our hero possessed abilities and energy far beyond his years. He further informed Bobby that he should have a room at his house, and that Ellen was delighted with the arrangement he proposed.

The gloomy, threatening clouds were all rolled back, and floods of sunshine streamed in upon the soul of the little merchant; but in the midst of his rejoicing he remembered that his own integrity had carried him safely through the night of sorrow and doubt. He had been true to himself, and now, in the hour of his great triumph, he realized that, if he had been faithless to the light within him, his laurel would have been a crown of thorns.

He was happy — very happy. What made him so? Not his dawning prosperity; not the favor of Mr. Bayard; not the handsome salary he was to receive; for all these things would have been but dross if he had sacrificed his integrity, his love of truth and uprightness. He had been true to himself, and unseen angels had held him up. He had been faithful, and the consciousness of his fidelity to principle made a heaven within his heart.

It was arranged that he should enter upon the duties of his new situation on the following week. After settling with Mr. Bayard, he found he had nearly seventy dollars in his possession; so that in a pecuniary point of view, if in no other, his eastern excursion was perfectly satisfactory.

By the noon train he departed for Riverdale, and in two hours more he was folded to his mother's heart. Mrs. Bright wept for joy now, as she had before wept in misery when she heard of her son's misfortune. It took him all the afternoon to tell his exciting story to her, and she was almost beside herself when Bobby told her about his new situation.

After tea he hastened over to Squire Lee's; and my young readers can imagine what a warm reception he had from father and daughter. For the third time that day he narrated his adventures in the east;

and Annie declared they were better than any novel she had ever read. Perhaps it was because Bobby was the hero. It was nearly ten o'clock before he finished his story; and when he left, the squire made him promise to come over the next day

CHAPTER XXI.

IN WHICH BOBBY STEPS OFF THE STAGE, AND THE AUTHOR MUST FINISH "NOW OR NEVER."

THE few days which Bobby remained at home before entering upon the duties of his new situation were agreeably filled up in calling upon his many friends, and in visiting those pleasant spots in the woods and by the river, which years of association had rendered dear to him. His plans for the future too, occupied some of his time, though, inasmuch as his path of duty was already marked out, these plans were but little more than a series of fond imaginings; in short, little more than day dreams. I have before hinted that Bobby was addicted to castle building, and I should pity the man or boy who was not — who had no bright dream of future achievements, of future usefulness. "As a man thinketh, so is he," the Psalmist tells us, and it was the pen of inspiration which wrote it. What a man pictures as his ideal of that which is desirable in this world and the world to come, he will endeavor to attain. Even if it be no higher aim than the possession of wealth or fame, it is good and worthy as far as it goes. It fires his brain, it nerves his arm. It stimulates him to action, and action is the soul of progress. We must all work; and this world were cold and dull if it had no bright dreams to be realized. What Napoleon dreamed, he labored to accomplish, and the monarchs of Europe trembled before him. What Howard wished to be, he labored to be; his ideal was beautiful and true, and he raised a throne which will endure through eternity.

Bobby dreamed great things. That bright picture of the little black house transformed into a white cottage, with green blinds, and surrounded by a pretty fence, was the nearest object; and before Mrs. Bright was aware that he was in earnest, the carpenters and the painters were upon the spot.

"Now or never," replied Bobby to his mother's remonstrance. "This is your home, and it shall be th pleasantest spot upon earth, if I can make it so."

Then he had to dream about his business in Boston and I am not sure but that he fancied himself a rich merchant, like Mr. Bayard, living in an elegant house in Chestnut Street, and having clerks and porters to do as he bade them. A great many young men dream such things, and though they seem a little silly when spoken out loud, they are what wood and water are to the steam engine — they are the mainspring of action. Some are stupid enough to dream about these things, and spend their time in idleness and dissipation, waiting for "the good time coming." It will never come to them. They are more likely to die in the almshouse or the state prison, than to ride in their carriages; for constant exertion is the price of success.

Bobby enjoyed himself to the utmost of his capacity during these few days of respite from labor. He spent a liberal share of his time at Squire Lee's where he was almost as much at home as in his mother's house. Annie read Moore's Poems to him, till he began to have quite a taste for poetry himself.

In connection with Tom Spicer's continued absence, which had to be explained, Bobby's trials in the eastern country leaked out, and the consequence was, that he became a lion in Riverdale. The minister invited him to tea, as well as other prominent persons, for the sake of hearing his story; but Bobby declined the polite invitations from sheer bashfulness. He had not brass enough to make himself a hero; besides, the remembrance of his journey was any thing but pleasant to him.

On Monday morning he took the early train for Boston, and assumed the duties of his situation in Mr. Bayard's store. But as I have carried my hero through the eventful period of his life, I cannot dwell upon his subsequent career. He applied himself with all the energy of his nature to the discharge of his duties. Early in the morning and late in the evening he was at his post. Mr. Bigelow was his friend from the first, and gave him all the instruction he required. His intelligence and quick perception soon enabled him to master the details of the business, and by the time he was fifteen, he was competent to perform any service required of him.

By the advice of Mr. Bayard, he attended an evening school for six months in the year, to acquire a knowledge of book keeping, and to compensate for the opportunities of which he had been necessarily deprived in his earlier youth. He took Dr. Franklin for his model, and used all his spare time in reading good books, and in obtaining such information and such mental culture as would fit him to be, not only a good merchant, but a good and true man.

Every Saturday night he went home to Riverdale to spend the Sabbath with his mother. The little black house no longer existed, for it had become the little paradise of which he had dreamed, only that the house seemed whiter, the blinds greener, and the fence more attractive than his fancy had pictured them. His mother, after a couple of years, at Bobby's earnest pleadings, ceased to close shoes and take in washing; but she had enough and to spare, for her son's salary was now six hundred dollars. His kind employer boarded him for nothing, (much against Bobby's will, I must say,) so that every month he carried to his mother thirty dollars, which more than paid her expenses.

Eight years have passed by since Bobby — we beg

his pardon; he is now Mr. Robert Bright — entered
the store of Mr. Bayard. He has passed from the
boy to the man. Over the street door a new sign has
taken the place of the old one, and the passer-by
reads, —

BAYARD & BRIGHT,
BOOKSELLERS AND PUBLISHERS.

The senior partner resorts to his counting room
every morning from the force of habit; but he takes
no active part in the business. Mr. Bright has frequent occasion to ask his advice, though every thing
is directly managed by him; and the junior is accounted one of the ablest, but at the same time one
of the most honest, business men in the city. His
integrity has never been sacrificed, even to the emergencies of trade. The man is what the boy was;
and we can best sum up the results of his life by saying that he has been true to himself, true to his
friends and true to his God.

Mrs. Bright is still living at the little white cottage, happy in herself and happy in her children.
Bobby — we mean Mr. Bright — has hardly missed
going to Riverdale on a Saturday night since he left

home, eight years before. He has the same partiality for those famous apple pies, and his mother would as soon think of being without bread as being without apple pies when he comes home.

Of course Squire Lee and Annie were always glad to see him when he came to Riverdale; and for two years it had been common talk in Riverdale that our hero did not go home on Sunday evening when the clock struck nine. But as this is a forbidden topic, we will ask the reader to go with us to Mr. Bayard's house in Chestnut Street.

What! Annie Lee here?

No; but as you are here, allow me to introduce Mrs. Robert Bright.

They were married a few months before, and Mr. Bayard insisted that the happy couple should make their home at his house.

But where is Ellen Bayard?

O, she is Mrs. Bigelow now, and her husband is at the head of a large book establishment in New York.

Bobby's dream had been realized, and he was the happiest man in the world — at least he thought so, which is just the same thing. He had been successful in business; his wife — the friend and companion of his youth, the brightest filament of the bright vision his fancy had woven — had been won, and the future glowed with brilliant promises.

He had been successful; but neither nor all of the things we have mentioned constituted his highest and truest success — not his business prosperity, not the bright promise of wealth in store for him, not his good name among men, not even the beautiful and loving wife who had cast her lot with his to the end of time. These were successes, great and worthy, but not the highest success.

He had made himself a man, — this was his real success, — a true, a Christian man. He had lived a noble life. He had reared the lofty structure of his manhood upon a solid foundation — principle. It is the rock which the winds of temptation and the rains of selfishness cannot move.

Robert Bright is happy because he is good. Tom Spicer, now in the state prison, is unhappy, — not *because* he is in the state prison, but because the evil passions of his nature are at war with the peace of his soul. He has fed the good that was within him up straw and husks, and starved it out. He is a body only; the soul is dead in trespasses and sin. He loves no one, and no one loves him.

During the past summer, Mr. Bright and his lady took a journey "down east." Annie insisted upon visiting the State Reform School; and her husband drove through the forest by which he had made his escape on that eventful night. Afterwards they called upon Sam Ray, who had been "dead sure that Bobby would one day be a great man." He was about the same person, and was astonished and delighted when our hero introduced himself.

They spent a couple of hours in talking over the past, and at his departure, Mr. Bright made him a handsome present in such a delicate manner that he could not help accepting it.

Squire Lee is still as hale and hearty as ever, and is never so happy as when Annie and her husband come to Riverdale to spend the Sabbath. He is fully of the opinion that Mr. Bright is the greatest man on the western continent, and he would not be in the least surprised if he should be elected president of the United States one of these days.

The little merchant is a great merchant now. But more than this, he is a good man. He has formed his character, and he will probably die as he has lived.

Reader, if you have any good work to do, do it now; for with you it may be "Now or Never."

OLIVER OPTIC'S BOOKS.

THE BOAT-BUILDER SERIES.
Completed in Six Volumes. Illustrated.
Per Vol., $1.25.

---

1. ALL ADRIFT;
    Or, The Goldwing Club.
2. SNUG HARBOR;
    Or, The Champ'ain Mechanics.
3. SQUARE AND COMPASS;
    Or, Building the House.
4. STEM TO STERN;
    Or Building the Boat.
5. ALL TAUT;
    Or, Rigging the Boat.
6. READY ABOUT;
    Or, Sailing the Boat.

The series includes in six successive volumes the whole art of boat-building, boat-rigging, boat managing, and practical hints to make the ownership of a boat pay. A great deal of useful information will be given in this Boat-Building series, and in each book a very interesting story is sure to be interwoven with the information. Every reader will be interested at once in "Dory," the hero of "All Adrift," and one of the characters to be retained in the future volumes of the series, at least there are already several of his recently made friends who do not want to lose sight of him, and this will be the case of pretty much every boy who makes his acquaintance in "All Adrift."

OLIVER OPTIC'S BOOKS.

FAMOUS "BOAT-CLUB" SERIES

Library for Young People. Six volumes, handsomely illustrated
Per volume, $1.25.

1. **THE BOAT CLUB;**
   Or, The Bunkers of Rippleton.

2. **ALL ABOARD;**
   Or, Life on the Lake.

3. **NOW OR NEVER;**
   Or, The Adventures of Bobby Bright.

4. **TRY AGAIN;**
   Or, The Trials and Triumphs of Harry West.

5. **POOR AND PROUD;**
   Or, The Fortunes of Katy Redburn.

6. **LITTLE BY LITTLE;**
   Or, The Cruise of the Flyaway.

This is the first series of books written for the young by "Oliver Optic." It laid the foundation for his fame as the first of authors in which the young delight, and gained for him the title of the Prince of Story-Tellers. The six books are varied in incident and plot, but all are entertaining and original.

OLIVER OPTIC'S BOOKS.

YACHT CLUB SERIES.

Uniform with the ever popular "Boat Club," Series, Completed in six vols. 16mo. Illustrated. Per vol., $1.50.

1. LITTLE BOBTAIL;
   Or, The Wreck of the Penobscot.
2. THE YACHT CLUB;
   Or, The Young Boat-Builders.
3. MONEY-MAKER;
   Or, The Victory of the Basilisk.
4. THE COMING WAVE;
   Or, The Treasure of High Rock.
5. THE DORCAS CLUB;
   Or, Our Girls Afloat.
6. OCEAN BORN;
   Or, The Cruise of the Clubs.

The series has this peculiarity, that all of its constituent volumes are independent of one another, and therefore each story is complete in itself. "Oliver Optic" is perhaps the favorite author of the boys and girls of this country, and he seems destined to enjoy an endless popularity. He deserves his success, for he makes very interesting stories, and inculcates none but the best sentiments; and the "Yacht Club" is no exception to this rule. — *New Haven Jour. and Courier.*

OLIVER OPTIC'S BOOKS.

ARMY AND NAVY STORIES.
Six Volumes. Illustrated. Per vol., $1.50.

1. **THE SOLDIER BOY;**
   Or, Tom Somers in the Army.

2. **THE SAILOR BOY;**
   Or, Jack Somers in the Navy.

3. **THE YOUNG LIEUTENANT;**
   Or, Adventures of an Army Officer.

4. **THE YANKEE MIDDY;**
   Or, Adventures of a Navy Officer.

5. **FIGHTING JOE;**
   Or, The Fortunes of a Staff Officer.

6. **BRAVE OLD SALT;**
   Or, Life on the Quarter-Deck.

This series of six volumes recounts the adventures of two brothers, Tom and Jack Somers, one in the army, the other in the navy, in the great civil war. The romantic narratives of the fortunes and exploits of the brothers are thrilling in the extreme. Historical accuracy in the recital of the great events of that period is strictly followed, and the result is not only a library of entertaining volumes, but also the best history of the civil war for young people ever written.

OLIVER OPTIC'S BOOKS.

THE STARRY FLAG SERIES.

Six volumes. Illustrated. Per vol. $1 25.

1. **THE STARRY FLAG;**
    Or, The Young Fisherman of Cape Ann.
2. **BREAKING AWAY;**
    Or, The Fortunes of a Student.
3. **SEEK AND FIND;**
    Or, The Adventures of a Smart Boy.
4. **FREAKS OF FORTUNE;**
    Or, Half Round the World.
5. **MAKE OR BREAK;**
    Or, The Rich Man's Daughter.
6. **DOWN THE RIVER;**
    Or, Buck Bradford and the Tyrants

Mr. Adams, the celebrated and popular writer, familiarly known as "Oliver Optic," seems to have inexhaustible funds for weaving together the virtues of life; and notwithstanding he has written scores of books, the same freshness and novelty runs through them all. Some people think the sensational element predominates. Perhaps it does. But a book for young people needs this: and so long as good sentiments are inculcated such books ought to be read.

OLIVER OPTIC'S BOOKS.

THE BLUE AND THE GRAY
SERIES

Illustrated. With Emblematic Dies. Each volume bound in Blue and Gray. Per volume, $1.50.

TAKEN BY THE ENEMY.
WITHIN THE ENEMY'S LINES.
ON THE BLOCKADE.
STAND BY THE UNION.

The opening of a new series of books from the pen of Oliver Optic is bound to arouse the highest anticipation in the minds of boy and girl readers. There never has been a more interesting writer in the field of juvenile literature than Mr. W. T. Adams, who, under his well-known pseudonym, is known and admired by every boy and girl in the country, and by thousands who have long since passed the boundaries of youth, yet who remember with pleasure the genial, interesting pen that did so much to interest, instruct and entertain their younger years. The present volume opens "The Blue and the Gray Series," a title that is sufficiently indicative of the nature and spirit of the series, of which the first volume is now presented, while the name of Oliver Optic is sufficient warrant of the absorbing style of narrative. "Taken by the Enemy," the first book of the series, is as bright and entertaining as any work that Mr. Adams has yet put forth, and will be as eagerly perused as any that has borne his name. It would not be fair to the prospective reader to deprive him of the zest which comes from the unexpected, by entering into a synopsis of the story. A word, however, should be said in regard to the beauty and appropriateness of the binding, which makes it a most attractive volume.—*Boston Budget.*

"Taken by the Enemy" has just come from the press, an announcement that cannot but appeal to every healthy boy from ten to fifteen years of age in the country. "No writer of the present day," says the Boston *Commonwealth*, "whose aim has been to hit the boyish heart, has been as successful as Oliver Optic. There is a period in the life of every youth, just about the time that he is collecting postage-stamps, and before his legs are long enough for a bicycle, when he has the Oliver Optic fever. He catches it by reading a few stray pages somewhere, and then there is nothing for it but to let the matter take its course. Relief comes only when the last page of the last book is read; and then there are relapses whenever a new book appears until one is safely on through the teens."—*Literary News.*

YOUNG AMERICA ABROAD.
FIRST SERIES.

A Library of Travel and Adventure in Foreign Lands. 16mo.
Illustrated by Nast, Stevens, Perkins, and others.
Per volume, $1.50.

1. **OUTWARD BOUND;**
   Or, Young America Afloat.
2. **SHAMROCK AND THISTLE;**
   Or, Young America in Ireland and Scotland.
3. **RED CROSS;**
   Or. Young America in England and Wales.
4. **DIKES AND DITCHES;**
   Or, Young America in Holland and Belgium.
5. **PALACE AND COTTAGE;**
   Or, Young America in France and Switzerland.
6. **DOWN THE RHINE;**
   Or, Young America in Germany.

The story from its inception and through the twelve volumes (see *Second Series*), is a bewitching one, while the information imparted, concerning the countries of Europe and the isles of the sea, is not only correct in every particular, but is told in a captivating style. "Oliver Optic" will continue to be the boy's friend, and his pleasant books will continue to be read by thousands of American boys. What a fine holiday present either or both series of "Young America Abroad" would be for a young friend! It would make a little library highly prized by the recipient, and would not be an expensive one. — *Providence Press.*

OLIVER OPTIC'S BOOKS.

YOUNG AMERICA ABROAD.
SECOND SERIES.

A Library of Travel and Adventure in Foreign Lands. 16mo. Illustrated by Nast, Stevens, Perkins, and others. Per volume, $1.50.

1. **UP THE BALTIC;**
   Or, Young America in Norway, Sweden, and Denmark.
2. **NORTHERN LANDS;**
   Or, Young America in Russia and Prussia.
3. **CROSS AND CRESCENT;**
   Or, Young America in Turkey and Greece.
4. **SUNNY SHORES;**
   Or, Young America in Italy and Austria.
5. **VINE AND OLIVE;**
   Or, Young America in Spain and Portugal.
6. **ISLES OF THE SEA;**
   Or, Young America Homeward Bound.

"Oliver Optic" is a *nom de plume* that is known and loved by almost every boy of intelligence in the land. We have seen a highly intellectual and world-weary man, a cynic whose heart was somewhat imbittered by its large experience of human nature, take up one of Oliver Optic's books and read it at a sitting, neglecting his work in yielding to the fascination of the pages. When a mature and exceedingly well-informed mind, long despoiled of all its freshness, can thus find pleasure in a book for boys, no additional words of recommendation are needed. — *Sunday Times.*

www.ingramcontent.com/pod-product-compliance
Lightning Source LLC
Chambersburg PA
CBHW031950230426
43672CB00010B/2116